TEN

POUND

POM

Niall Griffiths was born in Liverpool in 1966 and now lives and works in Aberystwyth.

His novels are: *Grits* (2000), a tale of addicts and drifters in rural Wales; *Sheepshagger* (2001), the story of Ianto, a feral mountain boy; *Kelly + Victor* (2002), *Stump* (2003), which won two Book of the Year awards; *Wreckage* (2004) and *Runt* (2006). There is also a work for younger readers, *Bring it Back Home*; a book in a series of Mabinogion re-tellings, *The Dreams of Max and Ronnie*; and two works of non-fiction, *Real Aberystwyth* and *Real Liverpool*.

Niall Griffiths also writes travel pieces, restaurant and book reviews, and radio plays.

TEN POUND POM

POM

NIALL GRIFFITHS

PARTHIAN

Parthian
The Old Surgery
Napier Street
Cardigan
SA43 1ED

www.parthianbooks.com

First published in 2011
© Niall Griffiths 2011
All Rights Reserved

ISBN 978-1-905762-14-9

Editor: Lucy Llewellyn

Cover illustration by Chris Iliff
Cover design by www.theundercard.co.uk
Typesetting by Lucy Llewellyn
Printed and bound by Gomer

Published with the financial support of the Welsh Books Council.

British Library Cataloguing in Publication Data – A cataloguing
record for this book is available from the British Library.

'Brisbane to Perth? That's a bladdy long way, mate.'

– Almost every Aussie I spoke to, in Oz, in 2007

'Thirty years? That's a bladdy long time, mate.'

– Ditto

'In the midst of all the constraints of a penal colony, the native-born had developed for themselves a sense of *physical* liberty and kinship with the landscape – like Australians in the 1950s, accepting all manner of censorship, Grundyism and excess police power, but feeling like the freest people on earth because they could go surfing at lunch-time.'

– Robert Hughes, The Fatal Shore, Vintage, 2003

DISCLAIMER: This book is not a work of fiction, but the reader is advised not to assume that every event recounted herein took place entirely within the confines of the real world.

GOING

As soon as the plane levels out the boy's nose explodes. Something gives in the tubes of his face, he feels a slight rupture, and twin crimson rivers leap out onto his shirt.

It's July 4th, 1975. BA flight 940 takes off from Heathrow Terminal 3, heading for Brisbane, Australia, with refuelling stops at Doha and Singapore. It's going to take an age. Everything the boy knows – school, city, friends – is receding into a smudge far below his seat, 24D.

There is a fuss around the boy. His mother and father are tilting his head back and holding tissues to his face. A stewardess is helping. The boy's brother (elder) and sister (younger) are looking at him over the seatbacks in front.

–Is he okay?, the mother asks.

–He'll be fine, the stewardess says. –Sudden change in

pressure, that's all. Happens all the time. Once his body adjusts the bleeding will stop.

But they're worried because they'd been due to fly four days previously but the boy had fallen ill and somehow they'd found a doctor at the airport and he'd ordered them to bump the flight and book a hotel and let the boy sweat it out for a couple of days in bed and that's what they'd done. Emigration – a big step, the biggest. To the other side of the planet. And the first moment of the divorce from the motherland is announced in lots and lots of blood.

NOW

Feel like utter shite. Hate flying when ill, drunk, hungover, and this was gunner be a crippler, twelve hours, horrible. Manchester–Singapore, straight through, with these sniffles and snots and aching kidneys and headache and sore throat and just general bleeuurgh-ness. Break out the nicotine gum. Twelve fucking hours.

–Wasn't like this when we flew last time, was it? Own telly and everything.

–There was just one big screen, remember it? At the bulkhead. D'you remember what films they showed?

–No. I remember coming back, it was *The Deep*, but not when we were going.

–Twelve fucking hours, tho. Hate long haul flights, I do.

–Well, it's either this or four weeks on a boat.

I watch three episodes of *Extras*. *Zodiac*, which convincingly dates itself in the early seventies when one of the characters boards a plane and is told that smoking is only allowed on the back six rows. Grumbling. *Flags of Iwo Jima*. An episode of a series called *Decadence: The Meaninglessness of Modern Life*, as it is particularly experienced in Australia, offering such statistics as 'Aussies work more than the super-affluent Germans', and '80% of Australians want to make a radical change to their lives'. A pundit talks about the 'democratisation of luxury'; how, today, you don't have to be rich to own Louis Vuitton or drive a BMW. Perhaps not rich, no, but you can't be poor, either. The programme attempts to air a discussion about the hollowness of manufactured identity and the voice-over states that 'the religion most Americans are experiencing is consumption... The mall is a cathedral to consumption, and we ape this in Australia'.

Something to look forward to there, then.

Bored to fucking tears. Not even halfway through. When's food coming?

THEN

The bleeding stops. The boy is told to sit with his head tilted back for a few minutes and this he does, feeling the scabs forming in his nostrils. The captain announces that food will be served shortly so those who smoke light up a pre-prandial cigarette. The plane flies through night-time and the boy doesn't know whether he is tired or not. It's night-time outside, but he's about to eat his tea. It's July, and back on the ground he'd still be playing out, on his bike, with friends and a football, in his old life. The plane has become like a house in the sky, a long narrow house shared with many others. A new place for him to live in.

Food comes; steak with tomatoes. Buttered vegetables. Croquette potatoes and fruit syllabub.

The boy finds a Spike Milligan radio show on his headset and listens to it several times over. He hears a joke that he doesn't, then, understand, but which will for some reason remain with him for the rest of his life:

In the morning, there was a heavy dew on the grass.
He'd been thrown out of the synagogue for swearing.

Somewhere over India he falls asleep. Wakes up with a lurch as the plane plummets through an air-pocket and looks around at the adults' terrified faces and listens to the captain's apologetic and reassuring tones over the Tannoy and falls asleep again.

NOW

All you do is sit on your arse and watch telly so why's it so tiring? Boring, too. Stupefyingly boring. Reading Robert Hughes's *Fatal Shore* and fascinated by it but the lack of visual stimulus batters the brain flat. Pancakes the brain. Through the window there is only blackness, soon to become daylight again when we cross over into another time zone. No trees or clouds or cars to see. All control over your own actions removed from you. Stale air that smells of farts. A steward wandering the aisles dispensing things is a cause for celebration; the hot towel is miraculous. Anything to break this monotony. When I get my Comfort Kit I'm almost weeping with gratitude.

An orange steward with a steely-grey quiff takes food orders. I look at the menu: Green leaf salad with bocconcini

4

and balsamic dressing, then a choice of chicken in white wine and prosciutto with polenta and greens or Greek style braised lamb with new potatoes and beans, followed by cheese and crackers and ice-cream. I'm excited. I'm bored and hungry and anyway I quite like airplane food; I like the space-management the eating of it requires, the little pots and packets. And sooner a broken bone, sooner botulism, than boredom.

I remember reading about a plan to cut travel-time to Oz to four hours or so; the aircraft would fly straight up, hover in the stratosphere while the planet turns, then re-descend once Oz was beneath it. Sounds a good idea. I last did this journey three decades ago and it takes the same amount of time now as it did then. Geologically slow, it seems. So bored I am. By the time we land the continents will have fused again. There'll be new mountain ranges, volcanoes and glaciers. Deserts where there were once seas.

What the fuck's bocconcini?

THEN

–How long will we be here for, dad?

  –Few hours.

  –Why?

  –Because they have to wind up the elastic band. The propellors in the engines are attached to a great big elastic band and they twist it up dead tight and let it go and that makes the plane move. When the elastic band's untwisted itself the plane stops moving so they have to stop and wind it up again.

  –Do we have to stay on the plane?

  –No, we can go into the airport.

The heat is like a fist. It punches the boy's breath from his lungs. He's never felt heat like this before and it frightens him a little; he feels trapped, oppressed. Breathing is difficult. Sweat pours. He sees palm trees. For the first time he feels a dizzying distance from what he knows but he's with his mum and dad and they'll keep him safe, they know what to do. On the tarmac, between the plane and the terminal building, he looks up at the stars and doesn't recognise them. They have an unfamiliar pattern.

–Bloody hell. Look at the muck.

The boy's dad puts a finger to a drinks machine and that finger sinks up to the knuckle in greasy dust.

–Look at that.

The boy looks up at his mother's face. She looks worried. Should he be worried too?

NOW

Christ – it fucking *gleams*.

8 a.m. Singapore time but midnight in my head and body. I'm confused and doddery and my eyes feel sandy. Singapore, tho; how it's changed – the airport building is all marble and glittering glass and tinkling water features, all of it scrubbed and shining and spotless. In the concourse, heading towards baggage reclaim, my brother elbows me and nods towards a beautiful woman pulling a heavy suitcase behind her as she might a recalcitrant dog. She has tumbling auburn hair, she's dressed all in black with one leg of her trousers rolled up to the knee, flip-flops on her feet.

–Think there's more like her in Singapore?

–I'm staying if there is.

I follow the signs for the smoking area. I'd heard terrible tales of the dictatorially over-legislated social climate of Singapore, that smoking was completely outlawed, that chewing gum was a punishable offence, but the little lit-up cigarette next to the green arrow was a good sign. I go up some stairs, through some doors and *OOF* – I'm outside. I remember this heat, this humidity, the brutal and instant impact of it. It comes back to me in a flash. The hot and wet towel yanked tight around the face, the tautening of the chest, the immediate trickle of sweat down the back. Nowhere else swelters under such heat. Southern Spain in a heatwave, central Africa, they're both a bit nippy compared to this.

I sit down by a lush green fern and roll a cigarette. The stone of the bench burns through my already sodden jeans and scalds my arse. I'm so tired. I put the cigarette in my mouth and try to light it but it's already soggy and useless and I throw it away and wipe my palms on my shirt and roll another and this one works. Inhale. Sigh. The *relief*, again.

THEN

In a souvenir shop the boy looks at a small toy bull, made with the fur of a real animal possibly, quite a realistic depiction with the flared nostrils and the horns and the dynamically-poised legs as if arrested in mid-charge. About the size of a kitten it is. The boy picks it up and instantly at his shoulder is a dark lady with metal in her face, rings and jewels, and a colourful cloak that covers her entirely except for her lean face all teeth and eyes:

–You love him? You wish to buy him?

The boy quickly replaces the bull and runs away. This place is too hot and the people are scary and everything he knows apart from his immediate family has gone away, has been left far behind.

NOW

Aircon like a cellular massage. Every atom coolly caressed. Every inch of skin sings. I speak to the cabbie:

–Is it always this hot, mate? All year round, like?

–Yes yes.

–Don't you have a winter?

–Yes yes.

–What's that like?

–This, but rain. All winter rain rain but every day hot hot.

We drive through traffic and tall buildings and palm trees into Chinatown. Street-stalls selling food, I don't know what, all tubs of hot oil and flashing cleavers. Pull up outside our hotel and pay the driver.

–How much is that in pounds?

My brother works it out. –About twenty quid.

–God that's cheap. Cab from Heathrow into London and you'll pay four times that.

The few feet from cab door to hotel foyer is a Saharan yomp but the foyer is cool again. The heat in this place is unbelievable, a physical assault. I feel almost affronted by it.

The lady behind the desk is sweetly apologetic:

–Ah, very sorry but rooms not ready yet.

Ah shite. –Any idea how long they'll be?

8

–Half past one.

–Half *one*? But it's only half ten!

She smiles and shrugs. Her smile is very pretty and she seems sweet-natured but all I want to do is sleep.

–We're just off the plane. Twelve hours. We're exhausted.

–We wait for linen but I'll try hurry them. Please; you get coffee in bar. We bring it.

I'm so tired I can hardly move. My brother's eyes are bright red. He looks like he's suffering very badly from hay fever.

We sit on soft couches in the bar. Lean against our bags. Ashtrays on the table, I notice. Singapore, it seems, is more relaxed than Britain, in certain matters. I want to get out and explore it. But I'm so, so tired. Coffee comes. I drink it. Wait. So tired my face slides off the skull and slithers down my chest to puddle up snoring in my lap.

THEN

Look; it's the Glitter Band.

Some men in platform boots and lurid spangly jumpsuits totter past the cafeteria. Big sideburns. They're laughing loudly and talking loudly and apparently enjoying the attention. Their lead singer isn't with them but thirty years later he'll make the news in, to say the least, an unsavoury fashion and the man that the boy will then be will flashback to this moment in Singapore airport when he was drinking orangeade and watching agog the sparkly men stilting by.

–Must be on some kind of world tour.

Clump, clump and shout and laugh away.

The boy's brother is leafing through some information he'd

been sent, on request, from the Australian embassy in London concerning Oz politics and aspects of culture. The boy looks at it but it doesn't make much sense:

LIBERAL Sir Charles Court
LABOR Mr. Colin Jamieson
COUNTRY Mr. R.C. Old

The country is called Mr. Old? And these are foreign names? Names from the other side of the world? There's a Jamieson in the boy's class at school, a David Jamieson. Or there *was*. That school doesn't exist for the boy anymore.

 –Dad, will there be tigers and things?

 –In Australia?

 –Bears and things?

 –No, says the mother. –But there'll be poisonous spiders and snakes. So you've got to be very careful.

 –In the house, even?

 –Maybe.

 –Will there be sharks in the sea?

 –Yes. So you've got to be careful there, too.

 A group of black giraffes glides gracefully past. One of them catches the staring family's collective eye and winks.

 –It's the Harlem Globetrotters, says the dad. –Bloody hell.

 They approach. They're very, very tall and they tower over the boy like trees and when they grin, and they *are* grinning, their teeth are very white. They speak to the family in deep voices and accents that amaze and one of them tries to engage the boy's little sister in conversation but she just stares with big and astonished eyes. A basketball rolls across high shoulders and spins on long fingers. They laugh a lot and make the family laugh a lot too. It's like magic, the boy thinks. These are people from a magic land and they can do magic things.

At some point, the boy falls asleep against his mother. He is woken up gently at their call for boarding and is steered in a trance onto another plane and he falls asleep again but wakes up when it takes off and he can see from the window the many lights, a sea of light, of the magic land that he's leaving. Where famous people live and miniature bulls and black giraffes who do miraculous things. One day he'll return to that land.

NOW

Oh Christ thank *fuck* for that.

Rooms ready. Linen found. Porter takes our rucksacks and we follow him wordlessly into the lift and down a plush corridor. When we try to speak it's like this:

–Ng?

–*Ngh*.

Jetlag has robbed our vowels. Or jtlg. Tony goes into his room, manages to croak: –Bar. Few hours.

–Ngh.

I go into mine. Big bed. Sleeeeep. Wake up thinking: Singapore Sling. I've *got* to have a Singapore Sling.

Up, shower, shite, shave, fag on the baking balcony where I deposit a tiny fragile cylinder of ash on the inch-wide railing (which I will find still there the next morning, so stagnant and unmoving is the air in this place). Back inside, fill the sink with cold water and plunge my face in it for a count of twenty then do it again.

I descend to the bar on springs. Sleep and a shower and

I'm a mustang. The first Sling tastes just as I imagined it would, like a lovely bellow of abandon, so I have several more then we hit Food Alley and eat the best sticky ribs I've ever had and then wander down to the riverfront, neon acrackle way up there in the haze, spotless city, glittering and agleam, the humidity something you have to wade through, dashing into shopping centres for the relief of aircon and bars to stand and sweat directly beneath the whopping rotors of the fans. The riverside area is all tempting dark bars and hawkers for restaurants every two yards, fried crab good good? Chilli shrimp? Salt-and-pepper squid, very fine sir? I drink lots of ice-cold beer and more Slings and am enjoying myself very much. I like Singapore a lot. Tony tells me:

–When I was in the marines, there was a kind of myth about Singapore about a building, a brothel like, called Four Floors of Whores. Each floor had a different kind of prostitute, y'know, straight, grannies, ladyboys. Don't know anyone who ever found it but it was kind of a legend.

–Four Floors of Whores?

–Four Floors of Whores, aye. Wonder if it's true. You hear all kinds of stories about these places. There's one about Hong Kong – Backside Alley. You go down a corridoor, apparently, a long wooden corridor with holes cut in the walls and arses sticking out of them. You choose your arse and pay and the arse is yours.

–To do what with?

–Anything you like, I suppose. You don't ever see the person, just their arse. Backside Alley.

–This true?

–Well, it's what I heard. You hear all kinds of stories about these places.

I drink more. Early hours, in a taxi, and the cabbie says:

–Where you boys go now? Hotel?

–To sleep, yeh. Knackered. Flew in from London the UK today.

–I take you boys somewhere.

–Where?

–Special place. Very special place.

–What, a club?

–No club, no. Better. Special place – Four Floor Whore!

–What?

–Four Floor Whore!

I turn around in my seat and my brother's laughing.

–D'you hear that? It exists!

The cabbie laughs with us and shouts: –I am fifty-five!

We go back and sleep. My sleep is deep and dreamless. Up, shower, coffee, wander, Buddhist temple, cab to Raffles Hotel for the lunch buffet. Another Singapore legend; I'd heard a lot about it. Travellers' tales. Always wanted to try it. By all accounts, the Raffles lunch buffet is spectacular. It's named after Sir Stamford Raffles, who founded Singapore in 1819, and it hosted its first guest in 1887 when, owned by the Sarkies brothers from America, it was 'basically a commodious bungalow', to quote William Warren's *Raffles Remembered*. It was extended in 1890, with the opening of the Suez Canal. Somerset Maugham visited, as did Noel Coward, Charlie Chaplin, other luminaries. Occupied by the Japanese during the Second World War but re-opened for business in 1946. The Singapore Sling was, apparently, invented in the Long Bar, probably in 1915, by a Hainanese bartender called Ngiam Tong Boon, whose adept hand I'd like to warmly shake. The hotel is all balconies and fragrant courtyards and grand ballrooms and marble balustrades and tinkling water features and by Christ it's posh. Sepia photographs show famous personages and colonial types in white suits and pith helmets and handlebar moustaches. How did they stand this heat, dressed like that? Much dabbing of empinkened brows with silken handkerchiefs went on, I imagine. Much spluttering too, no doubt. Tight white gaberdine buttoned up snug to the extravagantly bewhiskered thrapple in 80% humidity. I can almost hear the harrumphing. I say, Carstairs! What is it, Carruthers? Tell Gunga Din to fetch another gin, there's a good chap.

Forty shops in the arcade. Souvenirs and collectibles and gourmet food, that type of thing. I buy a notebook whose pages are watermarked with a stylised drawing of a louche bespatted fellow holding a cocktail glass with the words 'RAFFLES HOTEL – THE ONLY PLACE TO ENJOY A SINGAPORE SLING' beneath. And the buffet, God, the buffet... you pay your fifty-two dollars – about twenty quid – and are ushered into a cavernous room cooled by fans and assailed by smells and colours and the dash of diners and cooks. It's incredible. You pick up a plate and wander and fill it, eat, wander and re-fill, wander and re-fill, until you're a balloon. Half lobsters. Oysters and writhing sushi. Roast duck and kimchi. Roast lamb and spuds, beef stew, carrots, green beans, mashed potato and gravy for those who want to do a rainy British Sunday in the tropics. Curried pumpkin soup, pork loin, crab claws, ratatouille and goat's cheese pasta, smoked salmon, prawns, braised lamb shank, twenty different kinds of bread, runny and socky French cheeses. Literally hundreds of dishes, and you can try them all, as often as you want, for your initial plate fee, for as long as your guts hold out. All you have to buy is the drinks. And the puds! Tiny little artworks of chocolate and sponge and candied fruit and laceworked spun sugar. Large spikey fruits and odd nuts I don't recognise. It's brilliant. It's tremendous. It's wonderful. Apparently a tiger was shot beneath the pool table in 1902; he'd probably come in for the buffet. I could stay here for ever.

I am loving Singapore. That food and the heat insisted on a siesta, and sliming heavily back to the hotel I realised that my blue shirt was now zebra-striped with streaks of dried salt. From the sweat. A new one was needed, but the sizes were designed for Asian morphology, so even the XXL sizes equated to a British M; that is, for me, nipple-outliningly tight. I buttoned one up in the department-store changing-room and looked at myself in the mirror and could see, distressingly delineated, everything I'd just eaten at Raffles. Deeply unpleasant. I take it off and return it to the shop-girl.

–Too small still, I say. –Need big, big! Like a tent!

I find one, eventually, a short-sleeved billowing green thing which also, by that evening, sports foully fancy white stripes. Had it been black, I'd be looking like a piano keyboard. That night we end up in Little India, dirty and hectic and frantic and cheap and brilliant, worlds away from the skyscrapers and malls of the city centre. In the Prince o' Wales bar, the Cwrw Felinfoel *y ddraig goch* is up on the wall. The barmaid tells me that her boss is an Aussie of Welsh heritage; 'name Davies, his'. She asks me where I'm from, where I was born: 'Ah, you scouser!' There's a shelf of well-thumbed paperbacks by the door and I scan it and find a copy of my third novel and an anthology containing an extract from my second; next to my name on the contents page, someone had ticked it with biro and written 'YES!'

Singapore gets better and better. I'm loving Singapore. This is going to be a good trip, I think, the food and the booze and the colours and the sounds and revisiting my self thirty years ago, meeting my own ghost, childhood me, on the other side of the planet, those formative years and would I recognise that place or that boy growing up 12,000 miles from his home? Will I know his voice, should I hear him speak? The roots of the neuroses and obsessions that burn in *this* boy, now just past forty, will I see them? And if I do, will I know what they are? Around a booze-bath in Singapore's Little India, beneath a shelf bending with books with my name on some of them, a kind of delirium sets in and the planet contracts and expands as if it's taking deep breaths, as if it's tired, and I grow dizzy with discovery and possibility and every cell seems to hum in anticipation and I make for the riverside and drink still more in the salted haze and go back to the hotel and sleep and I'm liking Singapore very very much and then I get up and look at the ash still there on the railing and then I fly to Brisbane.

AUSTRALIA: BRISBANE

THEN

The ground isn't moving right. All those hours in the sky and the solid ground now feels to the boy like water, wobbling and unsteady, unable to be trusted. More heat, close and wet and heavy on his face. He's gone beyond tiredness, and confusion; it's as if all will and volition has left him and he is allowing himself to be steered and directed, his only response obedient indifference. This is Australia. He's in Oz. He drifts through the airport with his family and picks up luggage and gets into a minibus that will take him to the Immigration Hostel. On the bus, he meets a friendly, bearded Scottish biker called Stuart, and a large, round, pink man called Tudor George who bangs his head getting into the van and yells: 'Oo!' The boy's mother speaks to Tudor. Tells him that she doesn't feel as if she's in Australia and Tudor agrees:

–No, no. It hasn't quite hit me yet.

He says this with such jowly seriousness that the boy cannot help but laugh. Tudor and Stuart will, later, be allocated lodgings together, and each night Stuart will tell the adults in the shared kitchen how Tudor repeatedly tries to climb into bed or the shower with him.

–Ehs hamesick, eh sais. Tells ays ehs hamesick. Ah jist wish eh'd leave ehs alaine.

They are taken to Yungaba, the Immigration Hostel, a sprawling colonial-style building beneath a giant clanking steel bridge on Kangaroo Point, a mile or two out of Brisbane city centre, across the river. Whitewash and balconies and large-leafed plants and ferns and big loud flowers that make the boy think of dinosaurs. Strange bird and animal noises, whoopings, in this thick vegetation. Dripping heat. Their accommodation is an apartment with very high ceilings and partition walls that do not reach those ceilings and it is strange and big and echoey and very un-cosy. Mosquito nets can be unrolled from a box above the headboard to cover the beds but the boy will like that; it'll be like sleeping in a cave, or like being a spider in a web. Outside their block is a huge tree in which the boy's brother discovers an embedded Chinese throwing star. By that tree is a little kitchenette where the British and Irish adults will gather of an evening to eat toast and complain. Huge fruitbats fly over at dusk; the boy and his siblings count them, one night, and reach 250. There are lizards, and birds, of astonishing colours. Yungaba used to be a convent. Mince on toast, or 'shit on a shingle' as the Americans call it, is served for breakfast. The frightening matron hovers to deter people from second helpings and ensures that, during the day, while the men are out working, the ladies get to eat steak, while the men get pumpkin in the evening. The canteen's resident cleaner is from Liverpool and is called Thickbroom. That's his real name. The children quickly discover that fun can be had on clothes-lines; they're not simply cords strung between two fixed points, these are inverted pyramid-like structures, the likes of which they've never seen before, which can be hung on and spun. And they can be broken. And the shouting matron can be fled from, with much excited laughter.

The boy and his siblings settle in quite quickly. Children do – they have the knack of shrinking the world, of living entirely in the moment. It is discovered that empty soda bottles lifted from behind the nearby pub can be exchanged for money at the general store and one day they take in a bottle filled with large aggressive ants which scatter in their hundreds over the counter into the sweet display and the shopkeeper in his apron bellows at the children:

–Gerraht of it yer little pommie berstards!

More fleeing. The boy now needs to go to another shop to buy his Snowflakes; crumbly white chocolate in a shell of milk chocolate. Maybe with desiccated coconut on; the man the boy will grow into will be unable to recall.

The ants, and in fact the insects in general, fascinate the boy. Yungaba has a room with a ping-pong table in it and the boy is delightfully appalled to see the sea of scarpering cockroaches flee from the turned-on light in this room. Sometimes he and his friends dare each other to walk across this room in the darkness, to feel and hear the crunch underfoot, the tickling on their legs. And there's a spider, a palm-sized spider which lays its eggs on a leaf of the throwing-star tree; every day, the boy checks up on this spider to see if the eggs have hatched, until a local worker, Bluey, gleefully burns the egg sac with his lighter while his mates encourage him and laugh and the spider drops and scuttles into the grass and as boots stamp that grass the boy runs upstairs into his apartment and sits on his bed and cries for the spider and her never-to-be-born babies. He'll never forget the hysterical mob-mentality which accompanied the burning of the spider's eggs; the ugly joy and the base encouraging. Burn the fahkin eggs, Bluey! He's learning lessons, the boy.

A ferry takes people from Kangaroo Point over to the city several times a day. It's a brief journey; ten minutes or so. Less. The city is close; a good catapult could hurl a stone from Kangaroo Point through one of the windows in the skyscrapers that are shooting up, on one of which the boy's father is working. From the mud beneath the jetty, usually at dusk, thousands of crabs rise up and seethe in their thousands into the river. One day, the boy and his brother and their father watch huge, dark, triangular fins cut through the murky water. The boy's brother almost falls in; he loses his footing on the slimy decking and grabs onto the paling, just saving himself. Soon after that, the area hums with gossip about a man, an immigrant, who one morning filled his pockets with bricks and walked straight off the jetty at high tide. The boy is learning.

Eager to leave the hostel, the family moves into a house in the suburb of Inala. 53 Poinciana Street. Pampas grass in the garden. For a while, they will share the house with another Brit immigrant, Peter Higgins, from Oldham. When asked at school to write a piece about where he lives the boy will write that Uncle Higgy comes from 'Auldum', because that's how Higgy says it. This makes the boy's dad laugh a lot. But the boy likes how that word, as he's rendered it, looks on the page; it seems to resonate, pulse, although with what the boy cannot say.

NOW

Jesus, the security. Ridiculous. Huge signs everywhere with long lists of prohibitions. Don't do this. Don't do *this*, either. Australian airports might as well just have one massive sign saying DON'T. Easier, and takes up less room, to list the things you *can* do. Fuck's sakes. Been on the plane over ten bleedin' hours and I could do without this.

Fellers with ponytails and dogs hovering around the luggage carousel. Brogue-style shoes and shorts and tight socks pulled up to the knee. One dog sticks his head into the handbag of a Latina-looking lady and its handler perks up. Even his ponytail stands erect.

–Can I see yer passport, mate?

The bags shuffle around. I'm waiting for the wee happy lurch I always get in my breast when I see the familiar blue-and-black of my rucksack on the belt.

–Passport, mate.

I dig it out, give it to him to riffle.

–What you doing in Australia?

I tell him; revisiting, Ten Pound Pom, writing, etc.

–So yer a writer? What kind of writing?

–Journalism, reviews, novels. All kinds of stuff.

–What kind of novels?

–Superb ones.

–Yeh, but what kind?

–Science-fiction.

There's my bag. I see my bag, my friendly bag, shuffling towards me. I take it and my passport into Immigration Control.

–Yer a writer, are ya?

–Yes.

–What kind of books?

–Historical romance.

Stamp. On into Customs.

–So yer write books?

–Yes.

–What kind of books?

–Whodunnits. Detective stories.

And I'm waved big-fingeredly into Oz. I rejoin my brother in the busy concourse and marvel at its gleam; I don't remember it very clearly but what I do recall of Brisbane airport was a corrugated-iron shack or two and lots of claggy red dust. But this around me is all polish and glass and reflective steel. And I haven't seen Higgy in thirty years either but I recognise him instantly; smaller than I remember, of course, and with greyer hair, of course, but unmistakably him. Jeez: Higgy. Three decades on. How strange this is. He shakes my hand and I notice his lack of fingers.

–What happened there, Pete?

–Accident with a power saw.

Thirty years in Oz has not diluted his accent; still straight out of Auldum. We do the greeting thing and he drives us into the city. I'm knackered. My eyes are all gritty and all muscles moan. We pass through grimy suburbs, the typical surrounds of airports everywhere in the world, and enter the city at the Bradfield Highway onto the Story Bridge, from where I now get my first glimpse of Brisbane proper, its CBD, clustered glass towers erupting out of the river. The city didn't look like that in the seventies. My dad worked on the sixth skyscraper to be built in the city, lost now among scores of others. Yet I see the Custom House at the foot of the city, on the far bank of the river, and I remember it clearly – that green-domed roof.

Unchanged. And I recall, too, the rhythmic thumping noise that the cars make as they pass over the Story Bridge. A lullaby, that sound was. Strangely soothing.

–Anything like you remember it?

–God no. Not at all.

–People go on about Sydney, Higgy says, –but I prefer Brisbane, me. Sydney's plastic, but what Brizzy has is heart.

I can see the roofs of Yungaba below me to the right and another memory returns – the sight of those roofs in a child's eyes. The valleys between the gables and the thick green vegetation around the building but of course all has shrunk in the intervening time. But the smells and the noises of the birds in the branches have me shrinking too, limbs contracting, wrinkles smoothing out, hair returning to some parts and vanishing in others, scars unpuckering off my skin into the humid air. I am small again.

We go into the canteen, the kitchen, the apartment where we lived. Yungaba is now a Multicultural Ars Centre, so the immigrant/refugee spirit of the place still exists, and the room in which I and my siblings used to sleep is now the office of Bronte Morris, Director of BEMAC (Brisbane Multicultural Arts Centre). She's a nice lady, and she lets us wander around. I sit at her desk to write some notes, and if the spatial calculations of myself and Tony are accurate, then the desk sits precisely where my bed used to be. Thirty years ago, I snored and dreamed here, wrapped in a mozzy net, 12,000 miles from where I was born. I could sleep here again, now, so tired am I, just rest my head on my arms on the desk and drift peacefully off. I'm truly knackered. And I'm feeling big in my skin again; the smaller me doesn't fit. I'd burst his skin, were I to try and climb back into it. This is how it works, though; we shed skins like snakes. And I like being close to that boy, sitting here writing as he lay here dreaming. Lives pass in drips and drops and the years can be compressed in your hands like snow. Beginnings and ends don't, really, have much meaning or relevance; our notions of linearity are just theoretical, and open to disproof. None of them are irrefragable. None of them are uncontestably true. Maybe it's all just one immeasurable wheel and we jump off it and on it and off it and on it as it spins forever in space.

I pick up some information leaflets and go outside to smoke. I'd like to sit under the tree, the throwing-star, spider-egg-burning tree, but it's gone now; just a stump in the centre of a small car-park, that's all that's left. I find a bench by it and roll and light up and read a xeroxed extract from *Yungaba 1887–1987: A Century of Service to Migrants*, author not given. It tells me that 'Kangaroo Point, the garden suburb of the mid to late 19th century, was an ideal choice for the site of the new Immigration Depot, fulfilling Thomas McIlwraith's wish for a "barracks where immigrants would get a favourable impression in pleasant surroundings".' Hmm; that word 'barracks'. Interesting. A memory comes back; hiding behind a bush to flick the V at a group of boys I'd just had a row with and then turning to see the matron smirking at me from her balcony. The taste of pumpkin. (Why are the Aussies so big on pumpkin? The Yanks too, for that matter. Why do they both like pumpkin so much?)

'By the late 1880s... Brisbane's image was changing from that of an unlovely frontier town to a city of dignified buildings. A contemporary report described the architecture as a "mixture of handsome modern and sordid early".' Apparently, William Clarke of North Quay successfully tendered for the building of

Yungaba, with a quote of £14,285. Dates of construction and completion are 'a mystery' but certainly passed Clark's quoted deadline of fifteen months, largely due to wet weather; floods in 1887 'caused havoc', but the first immigrants were housed in Yungaba the following year, arriving on the SS *Duke of Buccleuch*. Not that it was called 'Yungaba', then; it was given that name in 1947, to welcome post-war migrants, and meaning 'land of the sun'. From the Maryborough dialect, apparently.

The place has been in my head for three decades and for the first time I have some idea of its history. Not that I can draw anything from it particularly, even if my head wasn't so fuzzy with jetlag; my family was simply one of many to have passed through this place. I was one of a hundred thousand boys or more to crawl breathing into bushes in search of birds or bugs. And Brisbane today? I flick through the 'official visitor's guide' for 2007. Discover that the Story Bridge doesn't have an 'e', and that you can climb, if you want to, to its 80 metre summit. Am asked: 'Have you ever woken up, looked outside and been greeted by a morning that has literally taken your breath away? You walk outside... the gentlest breeze wraps around you, the sun kisses you as if to say *good morning*, and the sky, well, heavenly could *almost* describe it. These mornings, these days, are commonplace in Brisbane. And they haven't just inspired the 24hr wearing of flip-flops and the planting of palm treed promenades. The blissful climate has had a profound effect on what we do and the way we do it.' Jeez, and they accuse the Brits of being weather-obsessed? At least in Britain we have seasons; in Oz, it seems, it's either hot or *dead* hot. On your Brisbane Dream Day you'd start the morning on the Kangaroo Point Cliffs and see the sun rising over the skyscrapers, 'not to mention the rock climbers creeping over the cliffs like cats'. Give that copy-writer an A for alliteration. Then you'd take a stroll through Roma Street Parkland, 'the world's largest urban subtropical garden', which is, apparently, 'paradise in the heart of the city'. Then you'd start walking at the 'ruggedly beautiful' Botanic Gardens and go north onto the Riverwalk, then 'swim, splash [or] wade your way' through South Bank Parklands, Oz's 'only inner-city beach'. Lord, this love of the littoral; an infatuation so strong here that they need to build a beach in a city only a few miles away from a real beach. Puzzling. Then the Brizzy Dream Day appears to fizzle out because the guide abruptly shifts to list other attractions outside the city, like North Stradbroke Island and Redcliffe and Moreton Bay, where I visited as a kid and to which I've also picked up a guide, which I also flick through; pictures of pelicans. And koalas. And more bloody beaches. And Steve Irwin hugging an elephant's leg before he got murdered by a fish. There's another leaflet called 'Greater Brisbane Drives: Get Out of Town!', but I can't be arsed looking through it, no matter now attractive that proposition might, in a few days, become. I'm tired and jetlagged and need a pint or a kip. Or a pint *and* a kip.

Tony and Higgy find me and we chat to a Serbian groundsman with whom I blether about Belgrade, a city I like, and then we go to the Bridge Hotel, the pub where my dad, and Peter himself, used to drink. All the grown-ups used to go there. Still do, of course, and now I can join them, because in 2007 now I'm a grown-up too. The beer works on the jetlag woozily and confusingly. There are plaques on the wall to a regular customer, a young woman, who died in the Bali bombings. I read them. Look at the pictures of her smiling face. A few pints and then the ferry over to the city, all bigger but all smaller than

I recall. Really needing sleep by now. There's the old post office, from where my parents used to ring relatives in Britain; a queue for the phone then a long wait for the connection and then a seven second delay on the line, that's what it used to be like. Now, of course, I text my girlfriend and the words bounce around the planet and reach her in seconds. The time that separates these two methods of communication is, really, too short. How fast we move. Are moving. Too fast, perhaps.

The main street is pedestrianised, now. In a cinema that used to stand here we went, as a family, to see *Jaws*. Blearily I recall a conversation with my sister outside the cinema after the film:

SISTER: That shark ate all them people.

ME: Yes.

SISTER: That first lady, there was only her top half left.

ME: Yes.

SISTER: That means the shark ate her bum. And there would've been poo in her bum. So that means the shark ate the poo.

Another bar, and Higgy tells us that he's been diagnosed with leukaemia, but it's now in remission, thanks, largely, to a new orally-administered drug. I'm shocked by this news, but he certainly looks healthy enough. Says he feels it, too. Tony's almost asleep on the table, as am I. Finding energy from some hitherto untapped well we drift around Brisbane in a daze then drive to the Gold Coast, Surfer's Paradise, and I fall asleep in the car and wake up in Alicante. Or what looks like Alicante. This was once a scruffy caravan park where we briefly holidayed and where I saw a UFO, us children outside at night, a huge blue-white ball trailing vapour between clouds. No longer; this is all tall tacky condos and traffic and tourism.

Some shacks still stand on the beach with skyscrapers in their back gardens; poor settlers bought these ramshackle dwellings some decades ago and are now multi-millionaires. We want to build a giant, tasteless tower in your back garden. Here's several million dollars. This isn't the Oz you once knew, blue.

We find a hotel suite. About ten floors up. I open the doors out onto the balcony and collapse onto the bed and am immediately deeply asleep until about 5:30 a.m., at which point I'm woken by the strangest dawn chorus I've ever heard, birds making noises that birds shouldn't be able to make, all falling whoops and rising shrieks and Swannee whistles and five-note airs, odd and alien and wondrous. I smoke a breakfast fag out on the balcony and stand smiling in the noises and watch the sun rise between the skyscrapers and over the blue sea behind them then I go back inside and wrap myself up in blankets and sleep some more. Wake happy. Move lodgings into Higgy's unit, which he shares, and which we had to wait to be vacated. We explore the Gold Coast, and I very, very quickly grow to loathe the place. It might not *look*, anymore, like 1970s Queensland, but Jeez it acts like it. See, in the seventies, Queensland was ruled by the virulent rightwinger John Bjelke-Peterson, who used his pet corrupt police force to 'suppress demonstrations with violence', and 'bugged political opponents, supported the South African apartheid regime, made law that discriminated against Aborigines, and relied on gerrymandering to keep power from 1968 to 1987'.* A fascist regime, indeed. He ran the state as if

---

*This is taken from a *Guardian* interview with the Brisbane band The Saints, written by Keith Cameron, called 'Come the evolution', printed in the edition of July 20th 2007. The Saints were a furious punk band who made a big impact in the late 70s with their singles 'I'm Stranded' and 'This Perfect Day'.

it was his own private fiefdom, accountable to no-one, deferential to nothing but his own greed. I don't know where Peterson's gone, but thank God he *has* gone, yet the Gold Coast coruscates with his legacy; the architecture would make Albert Speer engorged with pride, as would the ubiquitous prohibitions: No smoking (of course). No flip-flops. No singlets. No walking in a funny way. The doors of every bar or pub make you feel hugely unwelcome before you've even stepped inside.

And one night we'd arranged to meet Higgy in a surfer's bar so we turned up at the appointed time and met the manager at the reception desk, tightly T-shirted, slick-haired, self-satisfied, preening, strutting, peacocking prick of a man. Wouldn't let us in cos we didn't have ID. So we went go back to the unit, got our passports, returned. Members? No. Then you can't get in. But we can get signed in, can't we? Need a member to do that. Yes, we're meeting one inside. Yeh, but you can't get in without being signed in. Alright, what if one of us goes in and the other waits here? Much dithering and thinking. Okay. But the one who doesn't go in has got to stay here, at the desk. Tony goes in, I wait in the foyer, under this dickhead's gimlet gaze. Tony comes back out with Higgy, who signs us in and is interrogated by Bruce Hitler, who eventually condescends to grant us entry into his club, on the understanding that he'll be watching us like a hawk. Oh, he says, and points to me. You'll be taking ya hat off, n all.

Right, that's it. D'you really think I'm going to let myself be ordered to doff my cap to you? D'you really think that I'm so keen to get into your poxy little bar that I'll allow myself to be humiliated like this? Fuck you and your fucking smug strutting. Fuck you and the invisible carpets you're carrying under your arms and shite on your muscle T-shirt and your surfing tan and your Tom Cruise teeth and your orange glow and your fucking preening and shite in the hats I can see on the heads of your patrons through the doors in that overlit and overloud Euro-pop-thumping tacky theatre of self-congratulation that you call a fucking bar. Bars are supposed to be fun. What's going on in there is my idea of some kind of torture. Shove your fucking bar up your fucking Aussie arse and fuck off into the sea and I hope a bronze whaler rips you limb from limb you fucking idiot. I'm 12,000 miles from home. Australia's *not* the best country on earth and nor is the Gold Coast the best town in that country and nor is your fucking bar the best bar in that town. Shite on you. Fuck you and your surf bar.

–Bollox to this, I say to Tony. –I'll see yis later.

Tony comes with me to eat stir-fried beef and noodles on the promenade and then returns to the bar to fetch Higgy and I go back to the unit and watch a documentary on Palestine; Gaza Strip kids and Israeli kids are filmed meeting each other. It's touching and makes me think that only the fact of our growing up forestalls the establishment of peace in the world. Nothing else, just that.

Still seething, I take Higgy's swag-bag onto the balcony so as to sleep in the cool air and give the other two a break from my snoring, and myself a break from them whacking me with pillows to stop me snoring, and, truth be told, from their snoring, too. Below me, suspended between two trees, a spider dangles, its spread legs the span of saucer. Maybe, in the night, he'll crawl up onto the balcony and bite my face as I sleep. Fucking Australia.

In the morning, I ask Tony what he thought of the surf bar.

–Shite, he says. –Full of Bet Lynch lookalikes, only with less class.

THEN

At school, the boy and his British friends teach the Australian kids about porridge mines and scouse mines and haggis hunting. He draws a diagram of the scouse mine, a cut-away sketch showing the pit-head and the sunken shaft and the subterranean lake of scouse. A Scottish friend describes how the haggis run in herds across the hills around the town where he used to live, and he makes a drawing of one, like a potato with a smiley face and a pigsnout and sticky-out ears. The Aussie kids are fascinated.

Bullying begins, an extended and vicious bullying campaign against the boy and his siblings and other British and Irish kids. Every morning in the exercise yard, whilst singing 'Advance Australia Fair' during assembly, the bullies outline to the boy what suffering will be visited on him throughout that day. The boy's brother will remember the names of his tormentors: Colin Brassington and Ivan Dureki. These are children, true, but a level of sadism also extends to some of the teachers; one goads the children into catching cane toads, nailing them alive to boards, bloating their bodies with salt then slitting them open to reveal their working innards. Beating hearts, etc. The boy and his brother refuse to do this, and thus invite more bullying. The boy's brother reports Brassington and Dureki to the headmaster, who writes their names down on a fag packet.

The boy's mother takes him into the city, shopping, and they attend a street auction where a man holds up a velvet box and declares that what it contains is worth thousands of dollars but he's selling it for a fiver and the boy's mother buys it and of course it is empty. He's very convincing, the man.

As a family they visit Lone Pine Koala Sanctuary, Moreton

Bay, the Gold Coast (UFO), Beenleigh (famous for rum), Southport and Coolangatta. Wellington Point, Stradbroke Island, Bribie Island. At Currumbin, the boy holds a plate of chopped fruit as brightly-coloured parrots flock around him, perching on his head, his shoulders. The weight of them gathered on the plate strains and hurts his arms. At Bunya Park, the boy has his photograph taken holding a koala called Bill.

NOW

At the side of the highway that leads from the Gold Coast into Brisbane are large advertising hoardings. A local canvassing politician features regularly on them, sensibly-coiffured, shirtsleeves rolled up, arms folded, firm-but-fair facial expression. His caption simply reads: 'JEFF TURNBULL – A GOOD BLOKE'. How Australian can you get?

–You should be on one of those, Higgy, I say from the back seat. –Peter Higgins: a proper gobshite.

–Get fucked.

–Tony laughs.

We drive to Inala. This place had a bad reputation in the seventies and still has one now, but it seems to have improved, from what I can remember; it's cleaner, there's more shrubbery. There's less evident vandalism. Thirty years, thirty years. Hispanic-looking guys in baggy jeans and baseball caps hang around. Dogs abound. Thirty years. The same sun under which we age, all of us, every one.

Poinciana Drive, number 53. On the land where our house once stood there now stands a beige bricked, balconied place that stands out like an angel fish in a toilet bowl from the clapboard and corrugated iron dwellings that surround it. I feel disappointed and slightly sad, but I photograph it anyway, hanging out of the car window. I don't know what I expected to find, after thirty years, but some trace, however small, of my past presence would've been welcome. Yet I did walk this street, all those years ago. My little white Pommie knees. I was here, once. And am again. It's changed unrecognisably but I can feel myself all over it.

Inala West School, by contrast, is almost exactly the same, just painted a different colour. Blue – was it blue? Did it used to be blue? It's now a kind of creamy white. Tony and I vault the fence and cross the playing field where we once, and in a much smaller way, played footy (both Aussie rules and the proper kind) and cricket and rounders and prey to Oz kid bullies. We find a toothless groundsman and explain to him who we are and what we're doing there and he takes us up to see a teacher and we explain ourselves and our presence again. He's nice – lets us explore. There's my classroom. The wooden racks and shelves outside it where pupils stored their bags. Still there. It looks the same. Memories torrent back in. There's the window behind which I sat and through which Tony appeared, grinning, a large and long-tailed lizard draped over his finger. There's the assembly yard. 'Advance Australia Fair' and 'Waltzing Matilda' in the hot and heavy sun. The playing field, scrubby and dry. So strange, this is, to be back here. The other side of the planet and the other side of a life. All those years between then and now and all the living done in them and how all of it with its great weight depends on one thin hinge, ramshackle and small. Gone like a breath, really, slight and sustaining and fluttering and brief. The feeling is not too far removed from being bereaved.

The trip is getting interesting.

Back on the highway, heading up to Noosa, Higgy drives us through Moorooka.

–D'you remember the advert, boys? We all used to sing it together. D'you remember it?

And we do, suddenly, and we all three sing it, thirty years on from when we last did, two forty-somethings and one fifty-something now and less fingers and less hair and greyer hair and more scars and tattoos and muscles and height and bones and so much more living done since:

Moo-*roooooo*-ka!
Magic mile of motors!
Moo-*roooooo*-ka!
Service with a smile!

THEN

The boy and his family travel to Noosa Head for a day out. On the way there, they pass a giant pineapple by the side of the road and at Noosa the car begins to cough and splutter like an ex army major watching a documentary on glam rock, so it is taken to a mechanic in the town. *Watch this kids*, the mechanic says, and puts his finger to a spark plug and his tongue on the propped-up bonnet and blue sparks leap between the two. The boy's father roars with laughter. The boy stares at the fire that dances around the older human. They're of the same species.

On the beach called Squeaking Sands, the boy loves the sound the beach makes as he walks on it. His dad explains that all the grains are the same size so they produce a high-pitched noise when rubbed together. The boy likes this very much. Squeak, squeak. Men can make flame and a seashore can whistle.

NOW

–Look! There's that bleedin' pineapple! Still there!

And it is; house-high pineapple by the side of the road. Exactly the same. I didn't know what it indicated in the seventies and I don't want to know now but I'm happy that it's still there. Bloody stupid thing and what good is the world without such things?

–Noosa, says Higgy, who's driving. –It won't be like you remember it. Round about the time you boys were last there a mate of mine bought a house for eight thousand dollars and he sold it about ten years ago for ten million.

We drive over the Blackall Range Mountains, promoted on a map I pick up at a filling station as 'the Calm Behind the Sunshine Coast', which I sincerely hope it is, and can believe that it is, observing the seemingly-empty immensity that we pass through. So much space here. I'm knackered, today, very tired, after sleeping badly for three nights; I sleep better on the balcony than I do in the fiendish orchestra of apnoea inside the unit but I'm still woken early every morning by the dawn cacophony. It's a long drive to Noosa Head and when I get there I don't find it very exciting; money, beaches, tourists, big houses, usual stuff. Dull, except for the bush turkeys which wattle and scrat everywhere; them, I like. Funny little busy blue birds with velociraptor feet. I buy a take-away coffee from a kiosk on the beach and the guy takes the lid off the cup and shows me the liquid inside:

–That okay for ya, buddy?

–Grand, I say, and think: *Course* it's okay. It's black and hot and no doubt tastes of coffee. It's what I asked for. Why's he showing me my drink? –Thanks.

I sit with Higgy on a bench at Laguna Lookout. I came here too, as a child, but don't remember it. Uncle Higgy, as he once was to me, was also a Ten Pound Pom, landed in Oz in 1974 at age twenty-four. Went back to the UK in '76 but came back to Oz in '85, to Melbourne, because his sister lived there. After eight years there, he moved again to Brisbane in 1993, 'fell in love' (his words) with the Sunshine Coast in 1994 and has been there, in Mooloolaba, since. He's been a site manager for 14 years and makes a decent living; his brother, back in Auldum, a civil engineer, makes the same money as Higgy but 'it goes a lot further in Oz'. He got Australian citizenship in 1989 but he's 'still a Pom and a Pom right through', and if he *had* to – if he was forced to make the choice – he'd return to Britain. But he doesn't have to make that choice so he'll 'die in Oz'. He left the UK in the first place simply because he had the opportunity to see other parts of the world for a tenner – 'just adventurousness'.

Ah, Uncle Higgy. Now just a mate. I remember him with a bubble perm.

THEN

Curtiss Falls on Tambourine Mountain. Rainforest. The boy and his mother and siblings stand on a flat rock across a stream and the father takes a photograph and then the boy's mother starts to scream, terrible shrieks that set birds frantically exiting the trees and bounce back off the thick and stone-like trunks. The boy's mother is kicking her flip-flopped feet in a loud panic and the father is exhorting her to keep still so he can 'get it off'. The boy looks and sees the leech protruding from his mother's toe, it appears to be half-sunk in her flesh and wriggling its way further in and it gleams blackly sleek like a seal and a deep disturbance begins to writhe in the boy that such things could exist and his father whacks the leech away with the side of his fist and holds his mother and comforts her, laughing softly, not unkindly, at her hysterical reaction. *It's just a leech*, he tells her. *Just a leech. It's gone now.*

NOW

Mount Tambourine is a hilltop settlement of huge houses with startling views across the plain below and out to sea miles away, the Surfer's Paradise towers glittering in the far distance like upright shards of glass. Signs everywhere read DROUGHT AREA – SAVE EVERY DROP. Curtiss Falls is little more than a dribble, really, and not at all like the pacey mini-river I remember it as being, but that could be due to the drought. Still, I like the hanging hairy vines and the prehistoric ferns and the trees that loom huge and the bush turkeys and the humidity and the steam and the vivid flashes of lorikeets between the plate-leafed wrestling branches. And we find the flat stone on which we stood for the photograph and by which the leech attached itself to our mother's toe. I stand on the stone, in roughly the same place I'm standing in the photograph. Still here; three decades of the world's turning has not shifted that stone and has spun me around the globe back to it. Mighty magnet. I start to think about numenism, and how subjective that necessarily is, the impossibility of an unknowable localised ur-spirit when that very thing plays and wonders and worries like a younger self, how emotional attachment and investment must always mould the numen to one's own shape, but these are the thoughts of a man of forty and one of the opportunities I need and want, very much, to exploit here in this steamy jungle is a re-acquainting of myself with the boy I once was so I pretend he's standing by me, holding my hand, looking down into the clear and rolling water underfoot.

We stop at a bar for some food, driving back. I take an information leaflet and a cigarette onto the decking outside. A hawk, nearby, hovers in a thermal. His feathers are white. 'Tamborine Mountain Sanctuary' the leaflet says (no 'u', I notice), 'between the coast, the clouds and the country'. The Curtis Falls walk (no second 's', I notice) is praised as having 'an enormous strangler fig' and a 'causeway [that] takes you over the creek and little fishes are usually visible in the clear water'. The 'Quick-Facts' column tells me that Tamborine Mountain 'is a remnant of deposits laid down by volcanic eruptions 225 million years ago... Bush Turkeys and their eggs, Wallabies, Yams, Tamarind and Macadamia nuts are just some of the abundant bush tucker sort by aboriginal peoples for thousands of years on Tamborine Moluntain... At 550 metres above sea level it can be 5 degrees cooler than adjacent lowlands. It pays bring a jacket any time of year. With an average per year of 131 days with some rain, it is wise to bring a raincoat or umbrella' (*sic* throughout).

I wouldn't mind staying in this area for longer, really; the mountain towns with their restaurants and bars seem interesting, and I like Surfer's Paradise being at this distance, all those miles over there on the horizon. How wee it looks, at this remove. How puny.

THEN

A school trip to Early Street Pioneer Village – wells and log cabins and people wearing Victorian attire. How the settlers lived. Being led around the village the boy notices some large movement in a tangled bush and he crawls in there, no thought of spiders or snakes, no regard for the thorns that rip his skin. A dragon is hiding in the leaves. Small dinosaur, a spiked ridge of flesh on its back and a green wattle at its throat. Its claws curl like nail parings and its yellow eyes turn to the boy and a pulse beats lightly in its throat and a heavier one beats in the boy and he slowly removes an Opal Fruit from his packet and offers it to the lizard. Ridged nostrils sniff. A tongue flickers out. Rubber lips open and close and teeth bite. The boy is absolutely absorbed, completely rapt. There is no thought in his thudding skull other than the assimilation of what he's doing, what is entering his eyes, this lizard chewing on the sweet, and the boy takes in the tiny chasms between every scale and the fine mesh of the skin and the silvery claws and the sickle-shaped shadows that mackerel the back and flanks and he wants nothing more in the world, just this.

–GRIFFITHS! Is that you, boy?

The teacher, glimpsed through leaves, jigsawed by twigs. Round red face and a muzzy and shorts and a shirt a bit too tight.

–Geraht of there now! That's a bearded dragon! Yer mad, lad! Take yer bladdy fingers off!

The teacher's bellow has set the lizard scarpering. No point, now, in remaining here, in these thorny bushes.

NOW

Saturday night in O'Malley's, the only pub worthy of that name on the Sunshine Coast. Mock-Oirish place in a shopping centre, all dark wood and green upholstery. Caffrey's on tap. Chris, a friend of Tony's from home, who is yearing-out in Oz and has arranged to meet us here, stands six foot eight tall, and I crick my neck talking to him. His girlfriend, Nickie. Another feller called Paul, from Sheffield, with a shaven head and arms so heavily tattooed that they look like colourful sleeves, a decent and friendly bloke whose appearance nevertheless riles the Aussie uniforms. Last week, he tells me, he was returning home with a bag of shopping, two guys grabbed him, one arm each, lifted him off the ground and ran him towards another guy who was holding a dog. *Sniff him! Go on, good boy, sniff him!* The dog sniffed Paul, turned away, the guys dropped him and walked off. No apology, no explanation, nothing. Plain-clothes policemen and ignorant bastards.

   –It's crap, Paul tells me as we get drunker. –This part of Australia... wish I'd never come. It's all clean and sterile. All of it's to do with health and wealth but there's no fucking pubs, no fucking music scene, no little bars to discover down dark alleys. Wish I'd never bothered. But I've got kids. It's a safe place to bring up kids, I'll say *that* for it. Nowt bloody else, tho.

   We're introduced to a gang of locals who someone – Nickie, I think – is acquainted with and they do the usual enthusing thing; lovely to meet you, what d'you think of Oz, etc., except for one stocky little feller who shakes our hands half-heartedly and says 'yeh yeh, nice to meet ya, yer all cunts', which makes me laugh, because I think he's joking, and it's a funny joke, in the context. Later, however, smoking outside with Chris, the group pass us and say goodbye as they do so. Shortarse swaggers up to Chris, the point of his bullet head level with Chris's navel, stabs a finger up at his face and says:

–You. I've just fucked your missus in the dunny.

Shocked, Chris says: –Not bothered. So's he, and points to me.

–Yeh, I say. –And she told me that I was bigger and better than you.

Shortarse mulls this over. Mutters to himself: –Bigger... better...

I watch the ponderous thoughts porridge themselves through his echoing skull; Pom calls me small of dick and bad lover. Tall Pom is not biting. But shorter Pom has made insult. What I do? Smash Pom? Me not like be told him bigger and better than me as lover of ladies. Me not like *him*. Smash Pom? Smash Pom! MUST SMASH POM!

–Come on.

His girlfriend drags him away. Pugnacious little prick. Shortarsed fucking swaggerer, nobody's fault that you were born to be small, deal with it. You're not going to grow anymore. You'll always be short. Cultivate some dignity and you'll be a much happier man.

Paul joins us. –Was he giving you trouble, that copper?

–He's a copper?

–Aye yeh. I know him. He's not one of the worst, either.

Put a shorty with a hang-up about his height in a uniform and all you're going to get is grief. Especially here, where whether you fit in or not is predicated on such narrow-mindedly tight criteria... I witness an arrest, later that night, not long after the episode with PC Shortarse; three big coppers pounce on a slight and dreadlocked young man, throw him to the ground so hard that he makes a thudding yelp, sit on him, scrape his face across the concrete, cuff him. Killing an ant with a bomb, this is. I have no idea what the young man had done; had too pale a skin colour, perhaps. Or coughed too loudly. But I doubt very much that it warranted such treatment.

I get very drunk in O'Malley's, because I must, and stop for a pie on the way back to my swag-bag and balcony. Eat it on a bench amongst pecking white ibises, facing the sea. This should be lovely. But it's very far from it. Surfer's fucking Paradise. This is a shite place. I can't wait to leave it.

THEN

It's a short boat ride to Coochie Mudloe island but the boy loves it. He loves travelling on water. He can't swim, yet, and actually being in water scares him, but he feels an attraction to it, a powerful tug, that sits in him and which he likes to safely satisfy by being a passenger on boats. He thinks of the cold dark depths beneath the hull. He closes his eyes and envisions a vast blackness with a tiny boat on top of it and on that boat a tiny him. Giant sharks and squids and whales cutting across that unfathomable deep.

The boy's family set up a little camp on the island, in one of the wooden huts on the beach. Sandwiches and crisps and lemonade. From this base, the boy explores the beach; he clambers over the shed-sized bleached-white treetrunk that the tide has carried in, he bodysurfs the waves close to the beach on a small piece of polystyrene foam that he clutches to his chest, he and his siblings build castles of sand and dig holes at the tideline. Many different types of bird catch his attention.

He bobs in the shallows on a rubber ring, spooks himself and his sister by pretending that a submerged rock with trailing weed attached is the severed head of a young woman. He searches for, and finds, crabs in the rockpools, and anemones and shrimps and small and colourful darting fish. When he's alone in the hut, he pretends to be a shark-hunter, like the Quint character in *Jaws*, called to the hut by the island-folk who are trying to persuade him into killing the shark that has been eating them. *It can detect our blood from two miles away*, a worried villager says. *Correction*, says the great shark-hunter, chewing on a fishpaste sarnie, one foot up on the wooden bench: *Five miles*. The shark's been terrorising the island for months; the islanders can't swim, they can't fish, even the supply-boat was attacked last week and overturned and all its crew eaten. *So you've got a big problem*, the great shark-hunter drawls. *What's in it for me?*

The boy loves Coochie Mudloe island. He misses it when he's not on it. He has his photograph taken sitting on the beached treetrunk, big and warty and gnarly chunk of near-petrified wood, and when he looks at this image in later life he will recall the sharp tang of the sea and the crash of waves into his body and the happiness and promise of the island, all salty and sunbaked and secret, the constant joy of discovery.

NOW

I'm excited, again. I can see Coochie Mudloe getting closer to me, over the waves. Magical land, again, over the blue sea. A leaflet on the boat tells me that the island's name means 'red earth' in the local aboriginal dialect; it was from there that the aborigines got the clay with which to paint their bodies during their mystical rituals, the equivalent of the Native American ghost-dance. There's me, Tony, Chris, and Nickie. I feel that pleasant thrill in my chest that I get whenever I travel over water; I've had that feeling since I was a child, and it's never left me. I've had that feeling for as long as I can remember.

On the beach, we watch a fish eagle circle high over the breakers. Nickie, a wildife photographer, gets her camera out and snaps away. The bird soars, pivots on a wingtip, turns and circles, its eyes remaining locked to the water, spiralling down lower until it snaps into a dive and snatches its talons in the water and rises clutching a silvery-wriggling, violin-shaped fish. I am amazed. I'm breathless.

I love this island. It's remained with me for thirty years. The wooden huts on the beaches are no more, replaced by tables under a free-standing roof. We ask a man basking in his garden what happened to them and he tells us they were burnt down, 'set alight by Briddish soccer hooligans'. We talk to him about the island, about holiday-house rents. He tells us that the water supply comes all the way from the Blackall Mountains, 'best warda you'll ever taste', and he holds up an empty glass which his wife wordlessly takes into the house and comes back out carrying a tray with several glasses of water on it. The average Aussie male needs reconstructing, but the water is wonderful; ice-cold and clean and clear and it makes my head feel full of mint.

The noise of a hairdryer comes up from the dusty street. A full-grown man putters past on a motorcycle the size of a child's trike, his knees up to his ears. Chris, all six foot eight of him, watches him pass with a slow turning of his head. The confusion of scale here is brilliant. I laugh a lot. An old and chunky dog befriends us on the beach, follows us everywhere. I don't recall much of this island – what I remember most vividly are the beach-huts, and they're gone – but I love being on it, nevertheless. But then we return to the jetty and instead of turning left we turn right towards the Melaleuca Wetlands and it all comes back; the trees flanking and striping the dusty track, the sunken wooden steps down to the beach and the rocks and pools at the tideline and the small waves and, yes, the large piece of driftwood, the tree-trunk, still there, exactly the same, just a bit whiter with the sun and the salt. The me of thirty years ago, he's everywhere here. I sit next to him on the tree-trunk, I overturn rocks with him and marvel at the scuttling life we reveal. I walk with him along the beach and we throw sticks for the old and friendly dog. I see a bar in the trees with tables outside and I want to take the young me over there and buy him a Coke and myself a beer and tell him what's going to come, what heartbreaks and wonders and joys and pains to expect. I want to talk with him and be with him but I see the ferry coming in. Fuck it. Don't want to go back to the mainland, even if it will be my last night in Queensland. Want to stay here, with me.

BETWEEN

THEN

The boy's father is making alterations to the family car, a big, spacious, white Holden station wagon. The boy watches. His dad drills holes in the car's superstructure, just above the windows, and threads curtain-runners through them then clambers into the car and attaches curtains to the runners. He carefully cuts a large foam mattress to shape, lowers the back seats down, and slides the mattress in. Straps cases to the roof, full of clothes and utensils and personal effects. Stores food and medicines in the car. The effective space-management makes an impression on the boy.

–Is it a long way, Dad?

–A *very* long way. Miles and miles and miles. Across mountains and a great big desert.

–How long will it take us?

–About ten years.

–Honest?

–I'm messing. About ten days.

The car has become a little house that can move. The tailgate is up and the boy can see inside and it looks cosy and secretive and snug with the mattress and the blankets and the toys. He's excited, the boy, excited about the adventure ahead and the fact that he's leaving Brisbane. He's grown to dislike Brisbane. Wants to leave it behind. Maybe Perth will be better. And maybe on the journey between the two cities there'll be kangaroos and koalas and fun and excitement.

–Can we go to Currumbin before we go, Dad?

–Haven't got time, son. We're leaving tomorrow.

–Can we go on the way?

–We'll see.

–I like Currumbin.

–I know you do. We'll see.

It's still dark when the family get up in the bare house. The car, the travelling home, waits outside. It's very early morning, May 1st, 1976, although by the time the final preparations have been made it's fifteen minutes past midday when they leave Brisbane. The boy's in the back with his two siblings although there's another one on the way, in their mum's belly, new human growing, unknown at that point to everyone.

NOW

It's a Britz van, distinguishable by the company logo of the colourful lizard stencilled on the side door. And the big 'BRITZ' above the side window. We pick it up at the depot outside the city, by the airport, on 11th June 2007. It's got a fridge and a stove and a microwave and a sink and a table and two beds and some overhead storage which can be turned into another sleeping space for a child or a very small adult. It's a bank holiday in Oz, not that that makes any difference to anything, except the machine in the office spits out my credit card.

–Aw Jeez, why? There's loads of money on that.

–You'll have to ring their central office.

–Now? Will they be open? It's a bank holiday.

The guy leads me into an office and shows me the phone. I call the number on the card and press for several options several times and I'm just about to boil over when a human voice asks me if they can help. I explain the problem. Seems the card was refused because it's a large amount of money to put on it in one go but they'll clear it and in about ten minutes I can go ahead and make the transaction. I go back to the reception area, explain the situation.

–Righto. We'll give it another go in a few minutes. In the meantime, what type of insurance are you needing?

–What types are there?

And he lists many. I switch off. I'm bored to tears and restless because I want to be off, on the journey, away from bloody Brisbane. Want the Gold Coast – that Southend in the sun – to be miles behind me. The trip ahead is huge and I want to get it under way but the guy's going on about various types of cover and telling us that we need bedding and a whole load of other things and I'm feeling slightly sick at the thought of what this is going to cost. Like buying a house, this; all these hidden extras. You need this and this and this and everything costs. Nothing comes free, or even cheap. Even the information pack, which, for some reason, is a compulsory purchase, costs extra. And you return the bedding at the other end of your journey but what you pay for it isn't a deposit, it's rent, non-refundable. You get bugger all back.

–And you're going all the way to Perth?

–Yeh.

–That's a bladdy long way, boys.

If he thinks he can tempt me with an 'I Crossed the Nullarbor' T-shirt for thirty friggin' dollars he's sorely mistaken. I pay, wince, go outside to find a bench to smoke on whilst the van is tinkered and dithered with. They're making an inventory of scratches and nicks and other tiny damages, I think, something like that. Uninteresting, anyway. Much more diverting is the 'Safe Driving Information for Australian Roads' leaflet, which is a tad terrifying; it recommends the 'Outback Safety Kit', at one hundred dollars rental, again non-refundable. A satellite phone at seventeen bucks a day. Truly terrifying. The stuff about animals and dust-storms and the like is quite exciting; it's the expense that scares me. And should a 'roo dart out of the bush, whack into the side of the van, wreck the door? The insurance doesn't cover that. You'd have to pay for a new door, a new panel, maybe even an entire new body for the van. So what's the point of this insurance? Why doesn't it cover the most obvious and, I'm sure, frequent form of damage?

Nothing for nothing in Oz. But fuck it anyway; I'm off. Across the vast red continent.

–She's all yours, boys. Enjoy yaselves and be safe.

Tony and I get in. Little house on wheels. Tony circles the car-park a few times to get the feel of the vehicle and then we're off.

–D'you know how many miles are ahead of us?

Shudder to think. That desert. Watched *Wolf Creek* a few

months ago and now wish I hadn't. Maybe we should try and get hold of a gun or something.

It's a bright blue day. First stop is Currumbin. I remember lorikeets.

THEN

The boy stands in a storm of feathers, a typhoon of noise and thrashing colour, red and green and yellow and blue so bright, eye-rippingly bright, and the frantic cacophony the birds make in their flocks thousands-strong cyclones around him, perched on his head they are and on his shoulders and arms and on the plate of fruit he holds outstretched getting heavier with the massed weight of the birds. There is nothing he knows here, no Liverpool no Brisbane not even any Australia, no long jaunt no family not even any him, lost he is in this mad hurricane of feathers and beaks and chattering. Only pulsing in the many rapidly flapping wings like light is his contentment in which everything, origin and present and future, falls away except for the exactitude and clarity of his need to be nowhere else but here.

NOW

Ey, look; it was founded by a feller called Griffiths. Wonder if he was any relation.

Alex Griffiths, the noticeboard tells us, 'in 1947... began feeding the local lorikeets to protect his colourful gardens. Before long, visitors to Currumbin found out about the birds flocking to the area to feed twice a day and one of

Queensland's oldest tourist attractions was born.'

Nice feller. There's a painting of him reproduced in the booklet I buy at the ticket office and he looks like a nice feller; swept-back silver hair, blue shirt, kind of a noble set to his face. I don't recognise the park itself, so changed is it; then, it was more or less just a small field, but now it's a small zoo, with walkways through large flowering plants and a small train chugging around with children on it and echidnas and Tasmanian devils and dingoes and wombats in enclosures. The koalas are entrancing; they sit low in trees and eat eucalyptus leaves and when I watch them they do a kind of double-take as if in surprise to find me staring at them. There's an odd intelligence to them, a peculiar awareness and alertness; I've heard that eucalyptus, when eaten in large quantities, has a narcotic effect, and I can easily believe that, watching these animals, but inside their louche stoned-ness there seems to be an active and inquisitive mind at work. Bizarre creatures.

I like Currumbin. All I recall of it is a sort of rapture as I stood in the centre of a mad blizzard of lorikeets. I remember the surprising weight of them on the fruitbowl, how my arms ached for a day. How calm and content I felt as the birds sat on me and shat down my back and screeched in my ear. If we want to feed them today, however, we'll need to wait for hours, which we can't do, not with a continent to cross. So we wander round and look at the animals and then sod quite quickly off.

Wonder if he was any relation. Could easily be. One branch sprouted over the Dee into Liverpool, the other over the planet into Oz. And there's an obvious shared passion for birds, although whether such things are hereditary is of course debatable. But still: I wonder.

We take the Pacific Motorway through Beenleigh and

Coolangatta and Mullumbimby and stop at dusk in Byron Bay, which holds a literary festival to which I was once invited but couldn't go due to prior commitments and, wandering around the place, am now glad I didn't. There's a tree full of lorikeets under which I stand and marvel but the town is all gap-year types in batik trousers and dreadlocks and uniform faux-Celtic or faux-Maori tattoos and the entire place reeks of parental indulgence and superannuated self-satisfaction. Home Counties accents batter my ears in the internet caff and signs lobby for coach-firms, excursions down the nearby valley on which you will see 'natural wonders' and 'authentic aborigines'. Authentic? For fuck's sake. Enjoy your gawp-year, all you Barnabies and Tristrams and Jacintas. Oh what funny stories you'll have to tell back in Richmond-upon-Thames.

Ballina, Lismore, Casino on the Bruxner Highway. I'm beginning to get some notion of the vertiginous scale of Australian distances; what looks adjacent on the map takes hours of driving to reach. The place is colossal. Mallanganee, Drake, Sandy Hill, Black Swamp. The incantations in these names. So many histories we're driving through. Our intention is to reach Armidale because that was where we made our first stop on the journey thirty years ago but we're deep into night by now and Tony is tired so we park up outside Tenterfield, on the edge of the Blue Mountains. It's freezing. I wrap my feet in woolly socks and my head in a bandanna and my body in a sleeping-bag and sleep for a few hours then wake and crawl outside for a pee in the before-dawn and I'm shivering so bad my teeth are a-chatter. Dull dawn rising. Frost on the grass and on the reef of McDonald's wrappers in the ditches. Back in the van, sleep more, wake early. Wash with baby-wipes. Drink water, eat cereal bar. Drive on.

Dundee is four houses on the river Severn, which here is a muddy dribble. A sign welcomes us onto the Bald Knob Road and we laugh. There are a lot of 'Knobs' in Oz, I am to discover. Already met several. And we're evidently in Celtic Australia because there is the Gwydir Highway and Shannon Vale and Glencoe and Stonehenge and Ben Lomond and, look, Glen Innes, which declares itself to be the 'Celtic Capital of Australia' on a sign next to another sign that says, on entering the town: 'Domestic violence is a crime. Please report it'. We stop here, in the car park of a kind of pan-Celtic theme park, with rings of stones and a mock-up of Excalibur protruding from another stone and a wall with holes in it containing separate chippings and pebbles brought here from far Celtic parts, including Llantrisant and Caernarfon and Blaenan [sic] Ffestiniog by Mrs Enid Watkins-Jones. There are stones from my mountain, Pumlumon. I tell myself that I'm not going to stroke them but my hand reaches up as if of its own volition and gives them a wee caress. All small towns in Oz, as they tend to do in the States, lay some claim to individuality, whatever that might be, but this is important, really, here; as the noticeboard in the car-park says, the town was set up to 'commemorate those early settlers of Celtic origin who helped to build the Australian nation'. All Celtic languages are represented here, both Brythonic and Goidelic; there's even a reconstruction of the Tynwald, a small hill surrounded by stone slabs to sit on. Kernow is here. Breizh. Of course there's also something here of the speciously Romantic and mystic, of Clannad and the kilt and the kindly old mam cooking cawl in the cottage in the cwm, but still there's a good core to this commemoration. It's okay. I approve. And Llangothlin, some miles outside, is a few clapboard houses and bleating sheep and drizzle in a cold wind. Low green hills. Close your eyes.

The New England Highway dominates this Celtic region of Oz. Cuts straight across it, separates Oban from Llangothlin. I wonder if that was deliberate? There's a hamlet called Wards Mistake which sets me off wondering, intrigued, but it's miles away down some barely-there road and no doubt when we get there it'd be little more than a shack or two so we continue on through Guyra and Tilbuster and soon, no, not soon, but eventually we reach Armidale.

THEN

The Highland Caravan Park. A sign with a piper on it in a kilt.

–Why's there a Scotchman on the sign, dad?

–Dunno. Maybe the feller who owns it is from Scotland.

–Can you only stay there if you're Scotch?

–Maybe. You'll have to say 'och aye the noo' and 'hoots' and eat neeps.

–What's neeps?

They drive in, park, rent a chalet for the night. It's small and cramped and the boy claims the top bunk, mere inches from the wooden ceiling. He goes with his father to the camp shop for food, basic food to feed the family; potatoes and baked beans and cooking oil. But there is no oil. The boy's father speaks to the man behind the counter and another man enters from the back room, a big man in glasses and a woolly jumper and a big grey beard with his hands in the pockets of his trousers jiggling the change in them and doing a funny little dance to the song on the radio. He stops and stares at the boy's father and nods at him and says in a strong Yorkshire accent:

–Lancashire.

–Well, no, the dad says. –Merseyside. Same area, kind of.

They talk. There is a chocolate bar on display. On the wrapper is a picture of green fields in mist and grazing brown horses and it makes the boy think of cottages and log fires and dairies and farms and cosiness in the country. He wants the chocolate.

There is no oil so the boy's father buys a few tubs of margarine and they return to the chalet and the boy climbs up onto his bunk to be out of the way while his mother cooks. The smell of the melted margarine surprises him with its sweetness. Shortly after they've eaten they all go to bed and the boy imagines he's in a war as he falls asleep, a hero, protecting his family from armies of baddies and he wakes with a start to see wood so close to his face and they have breakfast and get back into the car and drive again into Uralla where they stop, briefly, to look at Thunderbolt's grave, which is when the boy becomes a bushranger on a strong and faithful horse which can leap across valleys and off mountains. It's not so much the chocolate the boy wants as the wrapper.

Tamworth. Goonoo Goonoo, which sets the children off singing 'I'm a gnu, how do you do?' Scone and Aberdeen, Scotland in Oz. A long day's drive across the Great Dividing Range whose landscape both exhilarates and scares the boy, and the sky turns dark and they enter the tiny scattered hamlet of Colo and find a caravan which the boy's mother says is 'grotty' but they stay there anyway and in the morning they leave the caravan and take a walk down to the river and now in daylight they can see where they are and the river gives up its mist like grey wraiths twisting slowly across the water and climbing the walls of the canyon, delicate tendrils that wave and ripple and are quickly gone.

NOW

It's still there, the Highland Caravan Park, still with the piper on the sign and the shop still in the same building and still with the meagre supplies, a few tins and a bread rack and a chiller cabinet. Some cooking oil, this time. We speak to reception and ask them how long the camp's been there.

–Ages, they say.

Look around, remember, drive into Armidale, park up, breakfast, Tony goes off to find an internet caff and I wander, buy some books, enter the fluorescent hell of the underground shopping centre and find a camping shop and buy a ten-gallon water jug in case the water runs dry in the van in the middle of the desert. Pretty enough frontier-style town, this. I'd heard a lot about the merits of Tim Tam biscuits so I buy some and eat them and am disappointed. Sit on a bench beneath a tree, smoke, read a local paper. Tim Tams are just like Penguins but with jam and stuff inside. One capuccino-flavoured which is so sweet as to be inedible. Need fruit. Can't keep fresh fruit in the van as it has to be given up at each state boundary because of the fruit fly so should stock up on it now, really. Can't be arsed. Eat another Tim Tam. Peach or something. Tastes of purple.

On to Uralla. The grave of Thunderbolt.

–Remember stopping here?, Tony asks, and I shake my head.

–Not really. Vaguely.

Just recollected heroics in my head. Bushranger Thunderbolt: robbed mail coaches and homes in the Liverpool Ranges District. Shot dead by Constable Walker in 1870, who first shot Thunderbolt's horse to draw the man out of hiding. Apparently, or so the sign says, Thunderbolt, for an armed robber, was a nice enough feller. These outlaws were once an Oz embarrassment; cruel, criminal, the convict strain asserting itself. Now, they're pioneering heroes, defiant, true rebels, exemplars of the Aussie spirit, untameable and beautifully wild. I'll see this most forcefully when I reach Ned Kelly country, but it's here, too, in Uralla; the well-tended grave, the iron statue at the road-side, Thunderbolt on his rearing steed.

Apparently there's a New England region in Oz as well as in the states because I'm in it and I've got a booklet that tells me so. It's 'renowned for its impressive historical buildings, aboriginal rock art and Regional Museums'. Main town is Armidale. 'Traditional landowners' were the Anaiwan people, who left their rock art in the Mt Yarrowyck Nature Reserve. White settlement began around 1830. Ben Lomond has a railway station, opened in 1884 and named after the area's highest mountain. Aboriginal name is Or-one geer, which means 'plenty white gum'. Wine is produced here; fourty-four growers and labels. Loads of national parks. Armidale is known as the 'Third City of the Arts', I'm told; regular events include the Women's Comedy Festival and the Pack Saddle Art Exhibition. There's a university, with 18,000 students. Armidale's population is 25,000, the 'city' has 'two pedestrian malls, surrounding these malls are many fine cafés with alfresco dining and wonderful shopping arcades, from large department store's to small gift shops and more'. By God, I can feel their pull. And it seems that an ineptitude with apostrophes is not confined to

British greengrocers. The town was named Armidale by John Oxley, first European to explore the area in 1818, named after MacDonald's castle on the Isle of Skye. Uralla, where I am right now, is from the Anaiwan dialect and means, maybe, 'ceremonial meeting place'. The booklet tells me that there are many antique emporia in the town 'for those who prefer fossicking in shops', and I'm impressed at the word. Always pleasing to see the resurrection of archaic terms. It's used again, though, in the section on Guyra: 'Imagine trying your hand at trout fishing in pristine streams, fossicking for gemstones, playing a round or two of golf.' Once is great; twice is a bit irritating. It's had the arse ripped out of it, now. And 'imagine playing a round of golf'? Why on earth would I want to do that? The desperately grasping nature of guidebooks never fails to divert and entertain. Imagine playing a round of golf. If I can't sleep, or if I require a vision of wasted time, then maybe I will.

We drive into Tamworth. This is the 'Country Music Capital of Australia'; more Billy Ray Cyrus than Hank Williams, I'll wager. It's also the 'Tidy Town Winner 1999', as was Llandinam, between Llanidloes and Newtown, back home. We stop for petrol in Tamworth and I eat a Golden Rough, which is a large coin of chocolate stippled with bits of roasted coconut, and the taste of it unleashes a torrent of associative memory, the force of which knocks me back a bit; I remember eating these when I was here last, in Australia, I mean. When the world was nine years old.

THEN

The family groups together under the sign that says 'LIVERPOOL RANGE'. The father takes two photographs which

will be sent home, accompanying postcards, to both grand-
mothers. Behind the family are hills and to the right is a wall
of thick and scrubby bush which, the boy feels, must go on
forever. These things on the other side of the world; echoes of
Wales and a place called Liverpool Ranges. And the road atlas
says there's a town called Liverpool, too, outside Sydney.
These familiar things on the other side of the planet but
familiar in name only so that in fact they only underline the
essential unfamiliarity of where the boy now is. Like looking at
a pair of favourite shoes at the bottom of a fishtank.
Confusing. They're only a couple of days into the journey,
they've only nibbled at the continent. It stretches before the
boy, too vast to imagine; not even his childhood talent of living
almost entirely in the moment can prevent the thought of that
distance from dizzying his head.

NOW

–There it is, look. It's still there.
    –Not the same sign though, is it?
    –No, but it's in the same place.
    –We park up and get out. I dig out the old photo of us
standing by the signpost and we hold it up next to the new sign.
There's the steeply sloping hill in the background, and is that the
same tree? We try to align the vegetation and the geographical
features but even allowing for thirty years' growth and
weathering we can't. Except the hill looks familiar, the main big
hill. And why would a new sign have been erected in a different
place? This, after all, is where the Liverpool Range begins.
    –Look at that.

A giant eagle sits in a nearby tree. It watches us watching it then launches itself off the branch and soars low over us, casting a shadow across our upturned faces as it checks us out then returns to its branch again, a thick branch which bends under the bird's weight. It's a huge bird. My heart thumped as it swooped low over my face. I'm sure that it was only ascertaining what we are, us two strange creatures in the alpha predator's territory, but I can't shake the feeling that the event is laden with some kind of spiritual significance. I feel slightly unsettled but thrilled; not merely at the pure magnificence of the bird but at the hint of a meaning that I can't quite grasp. Maybe it's no accident that, as my brother and I get back in the van, we simultaneously mention our paternal grandfather, nearly two decades dead. I don't know. But how mysterious this world is.

We drive through mountains. Low mountains, unspectacular as yet – they're not Welsh – but by God they go on. And on and on and on. The road to Colo River goes on forever and we're still on it when night has fallen and all we can see are the packed trees that densely line either side of the road. Just trees, and clotted black shadows beyond the reach of the headlights. Then some bright blue glow as we turn a corner and there surrounded by soot-black air stand three luminous blue crucifixes, each about thirty feet high, free-standing, star-bright in the thick black night. Bright, bright blue. I stand at the foot of one and hear the electricity crackling in it; the hairs on my arms prickle erect. My face bathed in the bone-white blue-bright light and all around me is blackness so thick that it'd be like swimming in ink if I left the thrown illumination of these bizarre and unexpected totems.

Christ but this is getting strange.

We park up in a layby in the darkness and sleep. In the morning we find the Colo River campsite which is closed for the winter months but we knock and a Kiwi feller answers. We tell him what we're doing and he agrees to show us around. He smokes American Spirit roll-ups with filters, as I do, and I like him. Colo is now a private park; all the caravans here are owned. It's a misty morning, as it was three decades ago, but in that mist the remembered beauty can be seen. That river, that rockface rising up. I recall walking down to this river, standing on this very beach in the morning after we slept in the caravan that my mum called 'grotty'. Which it was. I recall something of the wonder. And feel again this new wonder of encountering the younger me on the opposite side of the planet.

Christ but this is getting strange.

Drive on. Deeper into the Blue Mountains. The ground rises up. At Blackheath we park up and look out for Govett's Leap. Our youngest sister – who was born in Perth, as you'll discover – had been here a year earlier and advised us to visit it and, when we find it, we're glad she did; it's a suspended patio looking out over an abyssal drop between sheer cliff faces, spectacular, astonishing. Vast plunging space, tree'd escarpments far below immense slashes of bared stone. The waterfall off to the right is such a plunge that the water is gas rather than liquid before it reaches the valley floor all those skull-spinning metres below. I never came here as a kid. I think of the settlers, the explorers, encountering this for the first time; I imagine they felt as I do as they regarded this landscape, both stuffed with terror and bursting with possibility. It's vertiginous, immense. What lies atop those distant plateaus, across those great gulfs of blue and shimmering air? Oceans of space, here. I feel wonder.

At the gift shop I buy a Jacaroo hat and some information books and sit at a table with a can of cold cola and read them while Tony goes off to find internet access. I haven't checked my emails in days and I know that there'll be several that will require an urgent response but I'm enjoying myself here, it feels like a holiday, and I don't want to waste time at a keyboard so I sit in the shade of my new titfer and drink my cold cola and read my new books. Or flick through them, at least. I'll go online when we reach the next big city, when I've got a few hours to kill. Meantime, I read what Steve Parish has to say about this area in his *Discovering Blue Mountains*. What, no definite article? 'Sixty-five kilometres west of Sydney', he says, 'the Blue Mountains parts its shimmering veil to reveal the beauty of its sculptured cliffs and forested valleys'. Grammar, Steve, grammar; sort out your pronouns, lad. Think that should be 'sculpted', as well. Still, he's informative; twenty-four towns, apparently, occupy the main plateau. Chief settlement is Katoomba, the area's long been a resort for those Sydney-ites wanting to temporarily escape the big and nearby city. Another booklet, called *Layers of Time*, tells me that where I'm sitting is called the Evans Lookout, and Govett's Leap Creek is below me; to the left, at the end of the gorge, is Mount Banks, then Mount Wilson, then Mount Tomah to my right, and, after that, Mount Hay. Charles Darwin explored the region, in 1836. He stayed at the Weatherboard Inn, which is a brilliant name for a pub. Wish I could stay there too, if it's still there. And if I knew where it was. And could spare the time. The book doesn't tell me who Evans was, but it does tell me that Oswald Ziegler wanted to build a posh hotel on Evans Lookout in the 1960s, and to make a kind of Oz Mount Rushmore, with the faces of three explorers carved into the cliff face opposite, across the canyon, but the soft texture of the rock forestalled the project. Thankfully. Oswald the Idiot. Who'd want the power of that view spoiled and broken by a trio of vast blank faces? The States has a Mount Rushmore. The world doesn't need another one. God, what is it with some people? The unchallenged surety that the natural world can, and must, be improved if it's forced to take on a recognisably human form. God almighty. For those with the eyes to see, all faces are contained in the folds and nodules and striations and crannies of rocks. Nature offers the geoglyphs; take them. Don't try to impose your own. And who was this Ziegler? The thought of that question being asked at some future date no doubt led, in part, to his cliff-carving desires, but it's resulted merely in his memory being linked to megalomania, twisted vision and supreme arrogance. Where was he from? My third book, the *Glovebox Guide to the Blue Mountains*, written by Peter Meredith and Dan Fuchs, doesn't tell me, but it does mention that the Evans Lookout was 'named in 1882 after local solicitor George Evans'. That's all it says. Good Welsh name, or half of it is; I'd like to know more about him. This is by far the best book of the bunch; pretty well-written, full of maps and anecdotes and nuggets of information. Should I return here, this is the book I'll bring. It tells me that Blackheath is built at an elevation of 1,065.3 m, and has a permanent population of 4,119 (or it did in the year 2000). Sydney is just 133 km away. The whoops and trills and whistles I can hear in the canyon's trees below me are made by lyrebirds and whipbirds and currawongs. The place was named by Governor Macquarie, who first, in 1815, called it Hounslow (after the London Hounslow Heath), then forgot he'd done so and named it Blackheath (again after a district of London) on his way back through. The thicko. How can you forget seeing and naming a place like this? The book tells me, too, that Darwin also stayed at the Gardners Inn, once called the Scotch Thistle Inn, and that

William Govett used to love rolling huge boulders off the cliffs here, supposedly as a way of gauging their height, although he did admit that the activity was 'an amusement with me'. Fair play. And he was remarkably close; 160 m, he calculated. It's actually 161 m.

I'd like to hang about here, for a bit; wait until winter, when the snows come, get a room in one of the balconied hotels and do some walking through the gorges and across the plateaus and, at night-time, get rat-arsed in the Gardners Inn and come to Evans Lookout for a drunken gawp on my way to bed and see it all covered in snow under the blue moon. How would that look? I don't know, but I know I'd love it. Some bits of Australia are okay.

But that's it for Blackheath. Never came here as a kid, anyway, so it's got nowt to do with the trip. Just recuperation, after the hellish Blackpool-in-the-sun of the Gold Coast. Sightseeing and all that. Sydney's only about two hours away. I remember quite a lot about Sydney.

THEN

The family knew a couple, John and Margaret, who moved from Brisbane to Sydney, and it is they who they stay with whilst they are in the city, in their flat in the district of Vaucluse. It's a small flat, so beds are made up with cushions and blankets on the floor in the front room for the children to sleep on. The boy likes it; it's a nest, he thinks, beneath the bay window, through which he can look down on the revellers below, being as they are in Vaucluse's party area. One Saturday night the boy sees different coloured lights and people moving and dancing through those lights and he hears loud laughter and shouting and music and it looks all exuberantly abandoned and celebratory and suggestive of something good and bright about humanity. One day, he thinks. One day. There are things to look forward to in this life and this world. Plus, one afternoon, they go shopping in the Argyle Centre in the city by the bridge and they go to a bar and the boy wants a shandy but the barman has no more than a splash of lemonade left so the boy drinks a pint of more-or-less undiluted lager which is enough to get him drunk. Colours glow brighter and everything spins. The skin on the faces of the adults around him looks endlessly fascinating and their words reel with mystery and the hilarity and absurdity that underlies everything makes itself known and available. My God, thinks the boy, here is something extremely special. This stuff, this drink, this is something that is going to help him for the rest of his life. This is a gift from God. This is magical. This drink is a beautiful and secretive potion. The world trembles and hums in a curious pale blue light.

And, even through the sickness and sweating that come on later that night, still these words: This is truly magical.

They go to the Botanic Gardens and gaze in wonder at the huge orb-web spiders suspended between branches. They go to Coogee Beach. Bondi Beach too, where they witness large rats scampering through the litter on the sand of an evening and where they eat at the Double Bay Steak House after which, in the dad's words, they all 'get the wild shites'. On Coogee Beach the boy swims in the sea and, back on the sand, is surrounded by sea-wasps; giant jelly blue-bottles, they pop and hiss and spit and slither towards him with malevolent intent. He panics and leaps across them and runs to his mother. At

Botany Bay, John straps himself into a hang-glider, his first attempt at the activity, and is caught by a sudden gust and sent tumbling sideways to the bottom of the hill and cut and bruised and battered. The boy's eyes have that imprinted on them – the rolling triangle of canvas and the flailing shadowy limbs seen through it like a demented puppet play. Recovering from the accident that night, on deckchairs outside, John sips at his restorative tea and suddenly coughs and splutters and gags. A moth the size of a small bird had drowned in his mug.

Taronga Park Zoo. The Court House, Lady Macquarie's Chair. Parakeets and cockatoos and galas. Watson's Bay. At the Opera House, the children sit on top of the steps while their mother takes a picture, the building soaring, vast white clam shell, behind them.

–You're sitting too far apart, the mother says. –Get closer together.

They shuffle closer and squash themselves together like giggling sardines in a tin.

–No. Move further apart.

They do. Ten metres between them now. They find this very funny.

–You're going from the sublime to the ridiculous, the mum says, but takes the photograph anyway, and the picture will show them separated by several yards of space and tiny before the cliff-face sail of the building behind them and big beaming pleased grins on each of their faces.

Inside the Opera House is a huge painting depicting the hallucinations of a drowning man. Vivid squiggles and static starbursts, twisted faces, strange animals and birds on a deep purple background. It captivates the boy. He was born with a caul on his head. He is immune from drowning. These are images which he will never see and they're not too dissimilar from what happened in his head when he was drunk and they're not too dissimilar from what he saw of the partying people when he looked through the window of the flat in Vaucluse. Life can be this, that, way, even at the moment of its ending. Wondrous and colourful and immensely exciting. Thrilling and holy, even at the moment of its ending. One day the whole world will quake.

The boy likes Sydney. The big bridge and the surrounding sea and the towering buildings. He doesn't particularly want to leave, and when they do, and overnight at Orange in a caravan park and his sister wakes up in the middle of the night being sick off the top bunk and his dad runs to help her in the darkness and cuts his toe open on a chairleg ('CHRIST! Bastard! Me bloody toe!), the boy sees that as a sign. Should've stayed in Sydney. He liked it there. How the beer made people dance and how the people danced anyway. It is 1976.

NOW

Love that sight of cities, particularly unfamiliar ones, getting closer as I move towards them. The buildings growing bigger. So exciting; all that glittering glass and steel and concrete, and the narrow canyons between them which will contain bars and music and lights and people. There'll be a waterfront, full of dark dive saloons and salty air, there'll be people of many races and there'll be exhaust and neon and many different languages and many treasures to be found. Differences to be celebrated. Faces both hostile and friendly. Lots to discover, lots to explore. We check into the Palisades Hotel in The Rocks on June 14th.

This is one of the oldest pubs in Sydney, in one of the oldest European-settled parts of Australia. The bar is brilliant, dust and log fires and smoking permitted, the rooms basic as hell – bed, wardrobe, side table and that's it. Not even a telly. But it's clean and cheap with a wide balcony that overlooks the harbour, the arc of the bridge swooping above and the ships coasting underneath and the skyscrapers in the foreground and also beyond the river, the early-evening sunlight striking their heights. I already like this part of the city. It seems old, or at least as old as European-settled Oz can get. I don't remember Sydney looking like this, but then I don't remember much of the city's physicality at all, and no doubt it's grown and boomed in thirty years. The Nullarbor is getting closer to us, as is Perth, and those are the things that appear largest and nearest in my memory.

But The Rocks, The Rocks... this is the place where I first got drunk. My first ever taste of alcohol occurred here, in the Argyle Centre, which isn't there any more. So I get drunk in The Palisades bar instead and it's just as interesting and astonishing as it was all those years ago, the hum and hover in the head, raise the glass to your mouth and the world is one way then lower it and it's another. It's changed in those scant seconds of gulping. It's always the same in that it always changes. Each instance of drunkenness is different from the other, yet connected, somehow, links in a long chain of intoxication. Roundabout midnight, drunk, a taxi carries me under the bridge. I look up at it. Think nothing but a big bellow of approval, untranslatable. Fall asleep thinking; I've been drunk, now, on six continents. I know it's childish to feel proud of that. But now I've been on drinking sprees in six continents.

I have things to do in Sydney. A month earlier, back

home, I'd received an email from a feller called Ian Peddie, a native of Wolverhampton who was teaching at Sydney uni and conducting email interviews with contemporary British writers, his field of study. Would I mind answering some questions? Not at all, I said, but if he liked, we could talk face-to-face in a month or so. Great, he said, and he'll organise a reading for me at the uni. Bit of extra money for me. And my agent's assistant had put me in touch with a Sydney-based journalist, Geordie Williamson, and we'd exchanged emails and arranged to meet so I bell him and tell him to meet me on the steps of the Opera House, which is why I'm sitting there, slightly hungover, frowning at the rain that threatens to grow in strength, wondering if I'm sitting on the very same spot that my arse occupied thirty years ago. Going from the sublime to the ridiculous. I remember the laughter, and laugh a little again.

I like Geordie within a few minutes of meeting him. He's warm and learned and witty and interesting to talk to and he can drink like a thirsty fish. The sky opens and dumps oceans of water on us and continues to do so all day as we taxi over to the fish market where I gaze amazed at the pelicans and the bizarre, whiskery, spiny things on the slabs and eat fish and chips and peas in Doyle's famous restaurant, which are delicious, even without the vinegar. Geordie tells me that he grew up in Orange. My sister was sick there, I tell him. And my dad cut his toe open.

Tony joins us later and we drink a lot and then in the morning I have to chivvy him out of his room, which reeks of sweated booze and farts. He can't move. He's not used to heavy drinking. Welcome to *my* world, I tell him. You can bloody keep it, he says, and lets out more foul miasma.

We drive out to Bondi, past the Toxteth Hotel on Glebe Point Road. The Double Bay Steak House is long gone, replaced by a fast-food outlet, so we go for food in the Bondi Bay Hotel. It's still raining. It never stops raining. Battering downpour. Halfway through my shepherd's pie I feel ominous rumblings in my belly so I dash to the toilet and am both dismayed (at the mess) and pleased (by the symmetry) to discover that, again, and at thirty years' remove, I've got the wild shites in Bondi. This time, however, it's probably got more to do with the score or so of whisky shots I necked the night before than any kind of food poisoning. Still, nice to see that memory resides in the guts and arse as well as the head and heart.

Ian's with us, Ian Peddie, in Bondi. We'd met him in a pub the night before and I'd warmed to him instantly. A big man, shaven-headed, gentle giant, with that type of self-deprecating humour common in the Black Country which is always endearing. (He'll return to Britain not long after I do and we'll become friends. He'll have a heart attack in Sydney, after I leave, and jack in his job at the uni which will, allegedly, renege on his medical care.) He's been getting pissed off with Australia recently, and when he gives his reasons why, I nod and murmur in recognition at each one. Sydney's good, I like Sydney, but like most of the biggest cities in most countries, it's different from the nation of which it is nominally a part; it's more relaxed, more tolerant, less restrictive. Yet the experience of Queensland is still festering within me and the Oz propensity to over-legislate and control and forcibly modify the behaviour of its citizens and bask smugly in its own spuriously inflated sense of itself is still evident in Sydney, if to a lesser extent. And I'm only passing through; Ian's been living and working here. I've already seen enough of Oz to know that I couldn't do that. It would drive me crazy. That herd mentality. More on this, and of this, later.

We've got to get back to the city – my reading's scheduled for that night, in the university. At a pub close to the uni Ian interviews me while the rain furiously batters the corrugated-iron roof over the smoking area. It's ferocious, this rain, bouncing back thigh-high from the tarmac, hurling itself to earth as if in rage. The gutters are rivers, the roads wet running slicks exuding a thick and greasy mist of evaporation. Ian's recording our talk so we have to shout and I'm thirsty and drink quite a lot of Toohey's Old so that I'm half-drunk giving my reading, but it seems to go well; people laugh when I want them to, gasp when I want them to, throw up etc., and after it we return to the pub with some of the staff and students, one of whom attaches herself to Tony. She's pretty, if overly made-up, with pneumatic boobs, obviously silly-cone. Early forties. Quite a sweet person, but she has a way of fixing you with eyes unmoored and laughing hysterically at an unfunny comment for three seconds and then abruptly stopping. Serioushysteriaserious, like that. I feel a wee bit sorry for her, to be honest. She limpets herself to Tony and other students whisper to me that he must be careful with her. She's a poledancer in one of the city's clubs. Gangster-connected, or something. She's trouble. Not all there. Your brother needs to watch himself, here. I look over at Tony with my best expression of fraternal concern and he beams at me and gives me a thumbs-up. Oh Christ.

We go to Kings Cross, which is mad, but not in the sordid and lawless way of its London namesake; here, the chief impression seems to be of exuberance, not extortion. The prostitutes are astonishingly beautiful and they call us 'gentlemen' when propositioning us. *I don't go with working girls, love,* I tell one, *but if I did, I'd go with you,* which makes her laugh. No crack-raddled acned skin and morbid marasmus here, these women look healthy and well. I'd like to speak to them. Ask them about their lives, where they're from, how they ended up doing what they do for a living. We go to a bar called Baron's which has a late-night licence providing you eat so after one bite each of a hotdog downstairs we're allowed to go upstairs to a wondrous dimly-lit warren of rooms with sofas and tables and paintings on the walls, old, judging by their craquelure. I'm drinking gin. At the bar, the guy next to me asks the barman if it's true that the club is to close down soon and the barman sighs and pulls a blackboard out from beneath the bar which reads (and I'm quoting from memory, so this isn't verbatim, but you'll get the gist): YES, BARON'S IS CLOSING DOWN, LARGELY DUE TO A HUGE INCREASE IN RENT FROM GREEDY BASTARD LANDLORDS. WE'RE ALL AS PISSED OFF ABOUT THIS AS YOU ARE. DON'T WHINGE TO US. WRITE TO YOUR M.P.

That's a shame. This is a brilliant drinking-hole. We sit round a table, myself and Ian and Geordie and a guy called Steve who comes from Shropshire and whose lovely wife, Belinda, is the daughter of Liverpool-born parents. Some students are with us, too. My brother's off somewhere with the poledancer which is causing consternation:

–He needs to watch himself, your Tony. She's trouble, that one.

–I've told him.

–Should've warned him.

–I did. But he's older than me, he's a big lad, what can I

do? Can't bodily restrain the man, can I?

They tell me tales of the poledancer and her exploits. With each one I groan. Dread to think what Mum's going to say. I can imagine her look of despairing disgust.

This club, and the district of Sydney of which it is a part, has a messy energy and is possessed of a bursting life-force that I absolutely love. It seems free of that simmering underlying violence which characterises British cities on Friday nights, although Geordie tells me that it can be here, and I don't doubt it for a second. But I don't see it, tonight, wandering around the streets in the small hours; people are hugging, not hurting, each other. Buskers. Much music. Outside the fast-food places, people sway and eat stuff from paper bundles and no-one seems to be feeling the need to stab anyone else. Violence occurs here, I'm sure, but it doesn't appear to be an important ingredient in the atmospheric mix. This is a good part of Australia. I could stay here longer.

Later still, I'm in a cab with Tony, returning to the Palisades. The driver's from the Lebanon, listening in to our conversation. I'm telling Tony what the others told me about his poledancer, the scrapes and ruinations she's suffered and caused.

–They tell me she's bad news. Stay away.

–I know all that. Should've heard some of the things she told me. But in my defence –

–Bollox to 'in my defence'. You're digging a hole for yerself and not thinking cos Little Tony is doing the thinking for you. Stay away.

–Less of the 'little'. And in my defence, she *is* a pole-dancer. She can balance a ruler on her nipples and everything.

–You let the boy be, the cabbie chips in. –You jealous.

–Yer arse I'm jealous. I'm looking out for my brother, that's all. Why the fuck would I be jealous? I live with a woman at home who I love dearly and have no desire to sleep with anyone else and even if I did I wouldn't want in a million years to sleep with the woman we're talking about so why the fuck would I be jealous? Jealous yer arse.

–Ah, but me, I see a hole? He takes both hands off the wheel and smacks his right fist into his left palm. –I fill it (SMACK). See a hole and I fill it (SMACK).

So there we go, then. It's all sorted out, now. Thanks very much for that, Lebanese cabbie.

Sleeeep. In the morning I meet Felix, who I used to know as Boo, although Felix is his given name. He was the long-term boyfriend of the friend of a woman I used to go out with, and with whom I co-habited for a couple of years, in York. We've long since parted from these women and have different partners and lives now, his in Sydney, with children. We haven't seen each other for almost twenty years. Never close friends, we nevertheless got on well and liked and respected each other and it's good to see him again. He's hardly changed; few wrinkles around the eyes, some grey at the temples, that's about it. But we're both men now, with mortgages, careers, wives (common-law in my case), and, for him, kids. My past is threaded through Australia, from childhood to middle youth and, now, early middle age. The parabola of my life will always touch the antipodes, whether I like it or not.

Felix buys me breakfast. Bacon and eggs and toast. My booze-bloated belly protests at first but soon sighs and settles into grateful digestion. I feel energy returning. I'm leaving Sydney today, for Canberra. I talk with Felix about a thousand things. He likes his life in Oz. He likes Sydney. He doesn't know for sure but he thinks that he'll probably spend the rest of his life here. I'm happy to see him happy. I tell him of my misgivings about Australia, about its parochialism, the curtailed level of expansion in much of its citizens, its false air of 'no worries' acceptance. Felix tells me, echoing Steve and Ian, that Oz has pretty much of a tolerant attitude towards anything but the smallest misdemeanour; jaywalking, for instance, is seen as a vile and heinous crime. This makes a kind of sense, to me; I don't mean that the judgment itself seems rational, rather that its appearance in Australia, given the country's historical and ongoing socio-political climate, is logical and unsurprising. See, the convict strain seethes deep in the collective Oz psyche; it shouldn't, really – sons don't need to pay for the sins of the fathers – but it does. It smoulders in the marrow of the Australian Everyman. It means that he doesn't really trust others, that he feels anger and shame at not being trusted himself. The shallowness of the available history – an eighty-year-old telegraph station is seen as an ancient ruin – is reflected in the general mental attitude, which is happy to accept whatever lies on the surface and has an intense aversion to investigative endeavour. In Oz, history is not what you live; history is something other countries have. The aboriginal historical narrative is closed and removed, unless trampling over their temples such as Uluru can bring in the tourist dollar, and the aborigines themselves, when encountered in cities and towns, are either doing funny dances in face-paint for small change, or have been reduced to wretched drunks. Australian culture is, largely, at your shoulder, right in front of your nose; it's all immediate. By and large, it has no depth (of course, there are exceptions), which generates a kind of surface mateyness, which leads to a specious sense of solidarity, which produces a culture of snooping because if that mateyness wants to survive it needs the fuel of antithesis, for something to measure and define itself against; so revile the jaywalker, hold the smoker in disgusted disdain, sneer at those who want to wear a hat in surf-bars. The same thing is happening in Britain, albeit for different reasons; there, the meddler and the interferer and the snitcher and the twitcher of net curtains are being held up as examples of folk-heroes. They're nothing of the sort; what they are is nosey, pinched, dog's-arse-gobbed begrudgers who elevate themselves by inventing reasons to look down on others. And what does over-legislation achieve but more rage? Most people lead lives of low-level but incessant humiliation, swallowed by corporative interests and bent into shapes they don't want to adopt, that make them feel worthless and ashamed. Tonics to this have traditionally, and effectively, been lust and energy and exuberance, which is why places like Kings Cross exist and continue to sizzle; now, though, what used to be called 'going out' is stigmatised as 'binge-drinking', and is a socially irresponsible problem to sort out, and the demonisation of nicotine has meant that old men must stand like schoolboys in the rain outside their clubs and that pub-owners who want their patrons to smoke in the pub they own aren't allowed to let them. Humiliation pollutes the very arenas which were once temporary refuges from diurnal demeaning. Is it any wonder people are angry? That the average Brit sits on his sofa watching telly and screaming inside his skull? The solution is seen as simple: more laws, more restrictions, more curtailment and coercion. More prohibition. Which leads to more anger. More self-destruction and more violence against the person and more utter incomprehensibility of the notion of dignity. I see no way out of this; we seem forever stuck in this rut. We've sold our collective soul for the little throb of warmth we get at feeling, and being told, that we're better than others. This must be fought on a personal level, as a specie of defiance; don't allow these fuckers to emotionally impoverish you. Live life on your own terms, increasingly difficult though that's proving itself to be. Energy, energy. The world they've made will only be happy and complete when it's pounded you to paste, colourless and insipid. Don't let them do this. You must not let them do this. History has proved, repeatedly, that a people cannot be bombed into submission. Yet I fear that they can be legislated to death. God, I look into the future and see nothing but grey, flat, featureless, dull, uninteresting, soul-dead, grey.

Anyway. I say goodbye to Felix and we leave the city on the Hume Highway, aimed at Canberra. I think I'll miss Sydney. I liked it there. The roadmap tells us that there's a place called Liverpool close by so we decide to stop there for a wee bit. Just to see what it's like. How could we not? It's called Liverpool. On the other side of the world.

And it looks like the British Liverpool, too, or at least those parts of it which have been overlooked by the recent regeneration; Halewood, say, or Speke. Redbrick low-rise flats with the washing out, rusty railings, a busy arterial road, even a stoat-faced guy in baseball cap and shellsuit. Torrential rain. Graffiti. The resemblance is uncanny. Dumped supermarket trolleys. A few square blocks of gridded streets, one shopping precinct. And, oh, a museum. I go in. Tell the women at the desk that I was born in the British Liverpool, which leaves them markedly unimpressed.

The exhibits nearly all concern colonial massacres of the

local indigenous population. There were many of them. A settler named J. D. Lang called the area 'a dull, stagnant, lifeless sort of place'. Gloom grows as I wander around and continues to grow as I drink tea in the caff and flick through the local newspaper, the *Liverpool City Champion*. Front page: 'Deluge Disaster'. Tales of destructive floods and storms. Vandals wreck two buses belonging to Share Care, a local charity for disabled people. Stories about drug epidemics and death by overdose and the ineptitude of local MPs in dealing with such things. Speed appears to be the most commonly used illegal drug; a spokesman for the Youth Drug Support Team is quoted as saying: 'Heroin users are easier to manage because the drug tends to make them more docile, but amphetamine users are out of control.' Drug issues dominate the newspaper. The *Liverpool City Visitor's Guide* ('creating our future together') gives me some history; the area's original inhabitants were the Cabrogal people, who spoke Darug. They called the area Gunyungalung and populated it for 40,000 years. It became 'Liverpool' on November 7th, 1810, when Governor Lachlan Macquarie named it after the Earl of Liverpool, then Secretary of State for the Colonies. It's Oz's fourth-oldest town, behind Sydney, Parramatta, and Hobart, and the country's 'first free planned settlement'. Current population is over 155,000, and is growing quickly. Coming events, in 2007, include the Bent Jazz Festival and a Refugee Week. It has a Catholic Club, a Collingwood Hotel (Liverpool, UK, has a Collingwood Dock), a New Brighton Golf Club (Liverpool, UK, has a satellite resort of that name), many other correspondences; St Luke's church, a Mount Vernon district, etc.

The Liverpool Migration History Project has produced a booklet called *Memories + Fragments + Objects: An Alternate*

Narrative, which grips me enough to order a second pot of tea. The project is given to 'exploring the history of migration and settlement in the Liverpool area, [and] aims to trace migration patterns, settlements and indigenous histories through visual narratives'. It traces European settlement back to 1788, after the obligatory mention of the Darug and Tharawal peoples, when the first convict ships from Britain arrived, and it has a chapter on Ten Pound Poms, who 'earned a reputation for complaining, which those who firmly identified themselves as Scottish... escaped'. (Which isn't borne out by my personal experience; if you're from the UK, you're a Pom. Nor do I hear a great deal of complaining; in fact, I hear it mostly from native Australians who seem unable to stop complaining about complaining Poms.) Some had a right to whinge, 'adrift from all they knew and shocked by the conditions at hostels where they first lived'. There is mention of the alarmingly-titled Big Brother Movement, which was 'overtly committed to keeping Australia white and British', and there's a brief discussion of the 'New Australians', migrants who were encouraged to 'blend in by hiding their exotic cultural traits and diet [and] changing visible distinguishing characteristics like dress style'. Indeed, 'at the annual conferences of the Good Neighbour Council of NSW during the 1950s it was popular to have a "spot the Australian" competition in displayed photographs of migrants'.

Bloody hell. No wonder there's a drug problem. At the end of the booklet, though, there are brief character studies of twenty-three people who took part in the project, residents of the area born elsewhere. I like this. There are people from Iraq, Malta, Algeria, Fiji, Portugal, India, Serbia, Chile, Ireland, Greece, Vietnam, Yorkshire, others. An Iraqi guy says: 'The people of Liverpool they are good, actually multicultural, and the community here is establishing, takes all people. So I feel like at home.'

Just people trying to get by, that's all. I finish the tea, cold now, and we head for Canberra.

THEN

They arrive in Canberra at 2:30 p.m. and book into the Carotel motel at $28 a day. The dad feels ill and goes to bed to sleep it off and the boy and his brother and sister and their mother sit around the TV to watch the FA Cup final. Southampton beat Manchester United 1-0, which makes them cheer.

They stay in Canberra for a couple of days. It's a very peculiar city. There's a huge carousel in the centre, such as it is, and the man-made lake outside the civic buildings produces a display of multi-coloured water jets of an evening. In the Museum of Military History, an exhibit of the Cu Chi tunnels of the recently-ended Vietnam War captivates the boy's brother while he himself is enthralled by the First World War German tank which has the word 'Mephisto' painted on it and a stylised, fierce little devil painted below it. The boy wonders at the psychology of this; the playful, almost childishly cruel humour on a machine designed to do nothing else but kill people horribly.

Canberra's a government town, and not much else besides. Some years later, the boy will read what Gertrude Stein says about Los Angeles, that 'there's no *there*, there', and he will remember Canberra.

After Canberra, the Snowy Mountains and Cooma. Yarrangobilly Caves, which they explore. Dripping icicles of rock and underground lakes and a cool darkness and a creeping sense of panic outshone, just, by marvel at the place's strangeness. He likes these caves, the boy. They overnight at Tumut, in a cabin. Outside of this small town a flock of parrots bursts out of the bush and flies in front of the car and one of them bounces off the bonnet and over the vehicle and the children look behind to see the broken bird rolling and bouncing on the road, small colourful tattered bundle, shrinking, still and gone.

NOW

This is the capital city? It's like a dead zone. Apparently, the Australian government couldn't decide between Sydney and Melbourne as a capital so to stop the bickering they built a new city, from scratch, and indeed a new state. Designed by a lunatic, evidently, some foam-headed architect obsessed with concentric circles. 'Tis a bizarre place.

We drive around it on circular roads sunken between high grass embankments, every now and again catching a quick glimpse of a building and, once, a brief sighting of what looks to be a shopping mall, completely emptied of life. This is the world after the apocalypse. This is the world post-virus, when human life has ended, all of it's workings falling into first desuetude and then dry decay, reclaimed only by bindweed and hornets. Empty bags and fast-food wrappers blow like sterile tumbleweeds through the whistling streets. Not that I see any streets.

We reach the Military History Museum with twenty minutes to spare till closing, so only get to see both world wars. 'Mephisto' is now in storage, and if the Cu Chi exhibition is still there we don't get to see it because the doors are about to close. Outside, in an enclosed courtyard under a reddening sky criss-crossed by flocks of shrieking cockatoos, a lone bugler plays the Last Post. Happens every night, apparently, and is very moving. I admire this about Australia, the way it honours and reveres its dead. This is something to do with a young country constructing its heroes and mythology, for sure, but it's no less stirring and laudable for that.

Sun sets. We consider spending the night in a motel in Canberra but the thought of that makes me shudder so we head on. Such a strange place. Pass through Yass, back on the Hume. Coolac and Gundagai and then Tumut. Darkness when we arrive, full night-time. Hungry. Park up, go to a fried chicken shack. *Stuart Little 2* on the wall-mounted TV. Order fried chicken and gravy and roast potatoes and Tony asks if there's any vegetables besides pumpkin.

–Poys, the guy says. –Oi could do you boys some poys.

Peas it is. I enjoy the food. I'm hungry. After we've eaten we find a layby outside the town and park up. We're right on the edge of a busy main road in a scruffy part of the town and we don't really want to sleep here so Tony consults the map and recommends that we get on to Talbingo Lake.

–What's that?

–Don't you remember? Where we saw the fox chasing the rabbit?

–Oh I remember that. That's close, is it?

–Not far at all.

–Alright. Let's do that.

Onto the Snowy Mountains Highway, into the Kosciuszko National Park, across the Bogong Mountains. Can't see a thing except for a metallic glint of water under moonlight through trees so we park up by that glint and I get out of the van for a piss and it's freezing, I'm shivering, my teeth are actually chattering. I get back into the van and brush my teeth and put a woolly hat on and wriggle into my sleeping bag and soon I'm drifting off. Thirty years. This distance, this time. Last year when I was a boy.

THEN

–Quick, little bunny! Run for your life! Get away!

The boy's pulse is racing. They are standing at the top of a sloping meadow which rushes down to the lake, and on the banks of that lake across a dip in the field races a rabbit only a single paw-swipe in front of a sprinting fox. The animals aren't close but the boy can see the rabbit's frantically bouncing tail and the erect brush of the fox and the redness of his fur. Any minute now. Snap that fox will go, any second.

–Oh God, the boy's mother says. –He's going to get eaten.

The children are aghast, stricken, shouting:

–Run! Run, little rabbit! Get away!

The rabbit quick-darts at right angles but the fox mirrors every move, his body leaning sideways, his ribs close to the ground. This is it. He'll catch the rabbit. There will be mutilation and screaming and agonised death any second now.

–Quick! QUICK!

And then the rabbit vanishes. Just disappears into the ground and the dad says that he's found his burrow and everyone cheers. The fox paws and sniffs at the ground for a while then skulks away down to the lake's edge and is swallowed up in the rushes.

The boy's heart slows. He can actually feel his blood decelerating. The spectacle thrilled him completely, shook him with emotions that he can't quite name. His palms went wet and his mouth went dry and he felt a kind of heaviness in his bum and legs and all of his skin went tight and tingly. He's glad that the rabbit got away but he wonders now what the fox will eat. Wonders if the fox has got babies and if they'll now starve.

Later that day they stop at Blowering Trout Farm. Many circular chest-high tanks filled with fish, the water thrashing and boiling with the muscular bodies of trout. Many fish have jumped out of their tanks and are flapping and gasping and twitching in the mud, and the boy wants to put them back in the water but there are hundreds of them, all dying, drowning in the air. The boy wonders why they can't be fed to the hungry fox. Thinks that there is waste here.

NOW

I wake up and go outside and now in the daylight I can see where I am and in my memory this is always, exactly, how it has looked; the narrow dingle, the dip, the solitary tree, the lake behind it, and the thickly-wooded hill over that lake. All of this corresponds precisely to my memory. This is the exact spot, I'm sure of it. The running rabbit and the ravening fox. The sounds of shouting scared children. All of that happened here. Early exposure to the world's indifference, nature's violence. I've gone back in time as I slept. This is the exact spot.

Sunday morning. Cold. We drive on, needing a hot drink and food. A wash, too, but that'll have to wait; at least we've got some baby wipes. Essential items, if you're spending any time away from a shower or a bath; they at least give you the sensation of being clean. Blowering Trout Farm is still here but is closed, and there's no way of getting beyond the padlocked gates or over or under the chainlink fence, which is disappointing. The Yarrangobilly Caves are open, though, and after some tea and cake in the caff we go down into the vast yawning gob of their entrance, past a pink gala fast asleep on a railing. Can't say that I remember a great deal about these caves, beyond shiny spikes of rock and a feeling of low-level panic, and no memories gush back, apart from a vague one of an underground pond lit up like a night-time city seen from an aeroplane by the fairy-lights threaded through the stalactites above it, but that might've been a different cave system altogether. I ask Tony about it because he came here in 2005, with an ex-wife, but he's never heard of it. Ah well. That miniature underground city. It's somewhere in the world. Wish I could remember where, though.

More tea and a chat with the lady in the caff at the Visitor Centre, next to which are some houses which can be rented out and I go off, again, into a reverie about spending a winter there, writing, walking, sleeping, drinking. I'd love that. I think. Full of these reveries, I am. Don't know why; I'm perfectly happy with my home life. But kind of addicted to dreaming.

Later, we pass through Holbrook, with a sign on its outskirts declaring that it is 'Australia's Submarine Town', and sure enough it is; there's a huge sub half-buried in the ground. It's massive. What on earth? We stop, get out, look around and yes, that's exactly what it is; a huge sub half-buried in the ground. I'm reminded of the same thing at Wallasey, on the Wirral, the rusting hulk on the dockside still with its ack-ack guns on the deck, but that's a shipyard; Holbrook is hundreds of miles from the sea. What's it doing here? I ask a passerby and he says: –Don't know, ey?

Ah well. Fair enough. 'Australia's Submarine Town'; doesn't need any reason to be that, really. If it wants to have a huge U-boat half-buried in its centre, then let it. Curious. But a word about that 'ey'; Aussies tend to put it at the end of every sentence, whether inquisitive or declamatory. It's just a verbal tic, of course, and means less than when affected Brits do it, because they've consciously adopted it, but it's like the ornithological observation that the beauty of a bird's song in Oz is in direct proportion to the blandness of its plumage; the more lovely the song, the drabber the bird that makes it. Pretty-looking birds just squeal and screech. As if they know, somehow, that humans must be pleased and propitiated in some way, if not through the eye, then through the ear. They must make themselves useful, in some way, to humans. What's this got to do with the Australian 'ey'? Fuck it, I don't know. I'm rambling, ey?

Anyway, onward. Albury, Wodanga, Barnawartha. A tiny place called Everton. Beechworth and Glenrowan, Ned Kelly country. Poor old Ned.

THEN

There's something about Ned Kelly that provokes an emotion in the boy which he can only equate with liking something. He's been told that Kelly was 'a crook, a killer, a thief, a bushranger', but there are things about him... the armour, the last words, the last stand, the bullets pinging off his helmet, even the internally-rhyming name... the boy finds a part of him being drawn to all this, slowly, like a houseplant towards a window. He's heard the Fonz use the word 'cool' on *Happy Days* and he thinks that that word, in the way in which Fonzie uses it, might be applicable to Ned. He *thinks*. He's very young.

They stop in Beechworth to see the courthouse where Ned was incarcerated and sentenced to death. Dark wood and velvet clothes and coats-of-arms and plaques and everything else designed to impose and intimidate. Not much available info about Ned or his exploits, really, and the boy wants to know more so he asks his dad and his dad tells him what he knows but the boy wants more. Ned Kelly should be looming in his imagination like a bogeyman, with that blank helmet and those guns, clanking robotically out of the bush, but he's not and the boy is puzzled as to why. Wants to know more. He thinks he should but he doesn't have bad dreams about Ned. Wants to know why.

Back at the car, the dad discovers that he's locked the keys inside. He swears. The boy thinks that if Ned were here, he'd use his skills to break into the car and retrieve the keys and save them all but he's not here because he was hung at the age of twenty-four all this way from his home in Ireland and when he was asked if he had any last words he said 'such is life' and then they hung him and it's *their* fault that the boy's now locked out of his little moving house.

NOW

–How did we get back in the car? D'you remember?

Tony thinks. –I don't, no. Probably called the AA or whatever they had over here in those days. Got back in *somehow*.

Beechworth is like Deadwood in a beating sun, a frontier

town with covered arcades lining the dusty streets and wooden boardwalks and a New Orleans-style jazz band playing. It's very busy. Easy, here, to imagine sheriffs and shoot-outs and rearing horses and post-office robberies and stick-ups of stagecoaches. Almost unchanged from a century ago, it seems. There's a Scottish shop, oddly. A caff from where I buy a Ned Kelly Pie, which is a grin in a pastry crust; meat and gravy topped by an egg and cheese then baked. It's brilliant. When I return to Britain, I'll have my blood tested and it will show high levels of triglycerides, which will worry my doctor. I blame Australia's pies.

I visit the courthouse. Got to, really. How could I not? I'm alone inside it, and fascinated. I stand in the dock. I stand at the bench. When I go into the holding cells, a motion-activated recording clicks into operation and a croaky disembodied voice says: *Awroight, mate. You got a smowk?* The furniture and fittings are all original, including the dock and Ned's cell, over 140 years old. I buy a load of stuff from the souvenir shop; posters, booklets, copies of journalistic articles from the time of the Kelly Gang trial. WANTED posters, Ned's 'certificate of execution', which reads: 'I, Andrew Shields, being the medical officer on attendance on the execution of Edward Kelly, at the Gaol of Melbourne, do hereby certify and declare that I have this day witnessed the execution of the said Edward Kelly at the said gaol, and I further certify and declare that the said Edward Kelly was, in pursuance of the sentence of the Central Criminal Court, hanged by the neck until his body was dead.' All those bloody 'said's. Why do they have to do that, in legalese? I explore the town, guided by the 'Ned Kelly Touring Route' pamphlets which declare that Beechworth is 'Australia's Best Preserved Ned Kelly Town'. The Burke Museum houses Ned's death mask and a suit of Chinese armour that, apparently, 'sowed the seed for the Kelly Gang armour'. The Imperial Hotel, where Ned had a bare-knuckle fight with Isaiah 'Wild' Wright, and pummelled him.

All interesting stuff, as is the entire story of the Kelly Gang, and the position it's now assumed in the Oz collective psyche. One of the booklets says: 'Ned Kelly has never faded from our national consciousness. Indeed the passing years have seemed to build [his] legendary stature. Why? Perhaps because he had so many qualities ordinary Australians admire. He was a larrikin. Loyal to his family and ready to sacrifice himself for his mates. Represented the struggling classes. Thumbed his nose at the establishment. And he was fearless.' How different this is to the figure of national shame and embarrassment that Kelly was when I was last here, all those years ago. A thug, he was then; a killer of policemen; a street-brawler; a disgrace. As was his mother, Ellen, tinker-Irish, bred like a rabbit, Mick harridan carting her clatter of snot-nosed kids up to be thieves and rustlers. Now, according to a leaflet written by Noelene Allen, she's a 'woman of spirit and courage', who, when a child in Antrim, used to love 'exploring the beautiful rolling hills around her home searching for wild berries, bird's nests and flowers', who 'loved to sing and dance... A free spirit with a strong rebellious streak'. She came to Oz aged nine; her father wanted to emigrate to 'improve their position'. At eighteen, she met and married John 'Red' Kelly, from Tipperary, who'd been transported to Tasmania for stealing two pigs. Her parents disapproved of the union, so Ellen and John eloped to Melbourne and got hitched there. Their first child died at six weeks, but three more were born at their home in Beveridge, including Ned, in 1854. At the age of eleven, in Avenel, Ned saved a seven-year-old boy from drowning in the creek and became something of a local celebrity, whereas John began to drink heavily, dying from dropsy in 1866, widowing Ellen at thirty-three, with seven children. Ellen began to become known to the local constabulary and courthouses. She sold poítín from her house in Wangaratta and became pregnant, again, to a man called Bill Frost, who was court-ordered to pay maintenance, which he did until the baby died 'from diarrhoea' at fourteen months old.

In 1878 the troubles began; it was the year when 'all the misery started', in Ellen's words, when Constable Fitzpatrick paid a probably-drunken visit to the Kelly homestead on his own. You're probably familiar with what happened next, and know something of the Kelly narrative from this point on, and in any case I can't go into it here; it's freely available, from many sources. Ellen herself, though, outlived seven of her twelve children, and died, at ninety-one, in 1923. A grand old age. And, God, what a life.

I'm older now. I still think there's something of the Fonz about Ned, even though I realise that the 'natural' state of enmity between himself and the law that he frequently mentioned was a consequence of his rustling, and that his appeals to Irish emancipation from repression are deeply undermined by the fact that those whose livestock he stole, and the police officers he shot at Stringybark Creek, were all themselves Irish-born or descended. Still, the whole story's seductive, isn't it? The armour and that. And, by God, what a turn of phrase the uneducated and supposedly subnormal feller had. Look at this, from the letter he wrote at Jerilderie, seeking to explain his actions and defend his case: 'I have been wronged and my mother and four or five men lagged innocent and is my brothers and sisters and my mother not to be pitied also who has no alternative only to put up with the brutal and cowardly conduct of a parcel of big ugly fat-necked wombat headed big bellied magpie legged narrow hipped splaw-footed sons of Irish Bailiffs or english landlords which is better known as Officers of Justice or Victorian Police who some calls honest gentlemen.' That's brilliant. This letter, I feel, has been hugely instrumental in the rehabilitation of Ned from rustling thug to pioneering national hero. A lot can hinge on, and be ameliorated by, an interesting prose style.

But we need to get to Melbourne. Back in the van, back on the never-ending road. We pass through Glenrowan, which barely exists but for its Kelly connections; a bucket-headed statue of him stands as high as a house outside the general store. Plus there's Ned's Pizza Parlour, Kelly's Inn, and so on. Like those towns in mid-Wales which have built themselves around the red kite.

I need water and razor blades, and walk under the shadow of the giant Ned into the store. They have no blades, and no bottled water. I stay hirsute and thirsty.

THEN

The death-masks intrigue and appal the boy. The cold plaster behind glass and the set expressions on the faces, all serene, all peaceful, never, now, to change. He searches them for any sign, any hint, the merest suggestion of what it might be like to die but he sees nothing, just gently closed eyes and calm mouths, belying completely the violence of their going. But this is plaster; maybe if he saw the death-in-flesh... Why worry anyway? Death is something that happens to other, older, people. It'll never come for him. He's immortal. But one mask in particular fascinates him and holds him rapt; the facial features are much the same as the others' but this one, running from nose to nape across the bald skull, has a crimp like that on a Cornish pasty where some awful rupturing has been sealed. The accompanying placard tells the boy that this man, in a last desperate defiance of the authorities, broke free from the guards who were escorting him to the gallows, bent his head and ran full pelt at some cell-bars, splitting his skull open, killing him instantly. The boy thinks about that, cannot help but think about it; is there something noble about that death, in that way? An act of rebellion, the only possible one left. The terminal action of this life, to regain self-expression, to wrest identity back from the vast and faceless machinery that had swallowed it. And to split the skull like that – he must've charged the bars as fast as he possibly could. He must've been truly determined, with every cell of his body.

Nothing else in Melbourne Gaol impresses the boy as much as this death-mask does. It doesn't feel like a place of incarceration to him, with the laughing and running children and the tourists taking photographs and the light slanting in from the windows in the high ceiling and alive with motes. The gallows is on the third floor, and the boy wonders why it has to be so high. Beneath it, a long way beneath it, is a large drain.

The family stays in Melbourne for one night. They enter the state of South Australia on May 9th, Mother's Day, and they stop at a garage to fill up on petrol and the boy's dad buys a bunch of flowers for the mum. On a road entirely free of any signs of civilisation the back tyre bursts; from the back window, the children can see black rags wriggling in the road away from the car to turn and twist like snakes in the dust. The dad fits a new tyre, and buys a replacement at the next garage. 'Another $36 gone', the mum writes in her diary.

NOW

It's cold. Didn't expect it to be this cold. We get rooms at the Maroondah motel in Box Hill. The owner, a chirpy skinny feller who wears a hat like mine (maybe to hide chemo alopecia; he looks like he's recovering from a bad illness), takes a shine to us and gives us a discount. We ask him how to use the phones, me to call the UK, Tony to call Sydney.

–Calling the old women, ey? Bet you boys have sheilahs coming out of your ears.

We laugh. –We're doing okay.

In my room, I take a shower, which is like a hit of paradise, lie on the bed and watch Oz *Big Brother*, which is more or less the same as the British one, including the accents. Same eyes rapacious for fame, even of a brief and tawdry sort. Same attitudes – same eagerness to jettison dignity. Same mix of character types; the snob the sporty the thicko the babe the slightly-unhinged the shit-stirrer. How soul-crushingly fucking dull. I sleep like a log that night and catch a tram into town the next morning, which takes the best part of an hour. News that morning had declared that parts of the city centre around the Flinders Street area have been cordoned off whilst police investigate a fatal shooting; three shot, one dead, one a woman, the dispute probably domestic in origin. The shooter not yet apprehended, so the sky above the city is buzzed by helicopters. (Some days later, they'll catch the killer; he'd had a row with his girlfriend in a club, followed her outside, attacked her, then shot the man who came to her aid. Shot the girl too, but she survived; the samaritan died. Early 40s, young kids, on his way to work, killed because he couldn't stand by whilst a woman was assaulted. There'll be a photo of the killer in the paper; 'roid-swollen arms across his chest, one of them bearing the tattooed word 'CARNAGE' in huge Gothic letters. Dead eyes. Utterly dead eyes.) The Immigration Museum, with its advertised exhibition about Ten Pound Poms, shut. I was looking forward to visiting that. Find an internet caff and check emails instead. Drink coffee and eat a muffin. Explore a huge second-hand bookshop, buy the *Collected Prose* of Robert Creeley, and a Ron Hansen novel. I check the 'g's, of course. No Griffiths. Must've all been sold. I notice, in Oz, that used books aren't 'second-hand', they're 'pre-loved'. That's sweet.

A cold wind blows through the city's gridded streets. I meet a mad *Big Issue* seller. A *really* cold wind blows through the city's gridded streets. I like the mad *Big Issue* seller. She's got eyes like fruit-machine reels about to pay out and a laugh like a stack of saucepans falling onto a hard lino floor.

I remember the prison; I'm surprised, in fact, at how much I remember of it. The reproduction of Kelly's armour. The high gibbet with the large drain beneath it (for ejected blood and faeces and guts; sometimes the body would be wrenched from the head). The hanging model of the lead weight which basically drops an inch and is hoisted back up again; you press a button to make this happen. Which I do. The death-masks. A few cells have life-sized flat outlines of women-shapes made out of transparent plastic; I don't know why. But I like their lost and ghostly effects. The death-masks again. One in particular. Can't find it. I approach a guide and tell him what I'm doing there and what I remember and what I'm looking for.

Ah, yer after MacNamara. He's still there, ey. Cell thirty-four. Ya might not know, but after he did that, the governor at the time insisted that all bars be padded to stop it from happening again.

I go up to cell thirty- four. There he is – MacNamara. In his glass case with his skull still seamed. I've thought about you a lot, MacNamara, in the past thirty years. A lot. Wondered if I'd ever see you again, and now look, here I am, here you are, talking together again. You haven't changed a bit, MacNamara. Your skull's still split. You still look peaceful. What about me? Do I look now as I did then? Carry on sleeping, Mister MacNamara, carry on sleeping. Not like you didn't earn a good long rest.

Souvenir shop; guides to the gaol, some stuff about executions in the state of Victoria, 1894–1967. 1967? Bloody hell. That recent. The sixties swuang in many ways. Kevin Morgan's booklet carries the warning 'contains graphic references to execution by hanging', and the guy in the shop tells me that it's very gruesome. I take the books, and more coffee and cake, outside to sit in the sun at a table by the gaol's grand gates. Traffic roars and rattles past. The coffee's strong, the cake is sweet, the sun is pleasant, the wind has calmed, the sky is very blue. Kevin Morgan begins by debunking the myth of 'instantaneous' hanging, rightly pointing out the political imperative behind the perpetuation of that myth: 'any statement to the contrary would result in an electorate having to search its conscience[,] a discomfiting prospect for any government intent on maintaining office'. He writes that women would often have lead weights attached to their skirts so that they didn't ride up 'immodestly' when they fell. Some hangmen were clearly incompetents with a strong streak of sadism; one, Robert Gibbon, was a 'mentally deficient child-sex offender', who took over from a feller called Pauling after he (Pauling, I mean) fled the state to escape from his alcoholism and gambling debts. Gibbon was also installed as

Victoria's chief flagellator, but lost his job in 1909 when 'his mind broke down altogether. He hallucinated that naked girls were taunting him in the streets and, complaining to the police, declared that if nothing was done about the problem, he would begin hanging the girls himself.' A fine man for the job, then. Morgan outlines several case histories, people who suffered executions just as savage and vile and hideous as the crimes they were convicted of (and often much, much more so). It's depressing reading, a horrible glimpse into human coldness and numbness: 'The whole exercise of a hanging was seen as little more than a legally-sanctioned indulgence for one or two inquiring medical men in an experiment with ropes and weights and forces about which no-one seemed to know less than the executor himself.' I'd recommend this book to anyone who supports the re-instatement of capital punishment, except that I know that not even books like this one will deter them from their foaming need for vengeance. As long as it's not happening to them, they don't really care.

I'm so glad that hanging was outlawed. It has no place in the world. We'll kill the person who killed the person because there's nothing worse than killing a person, except when we do it, because we've made murder legal, for us (and, often, the death sentence was passed for non-lethal crimes). Disgusting. It must never come back.

Ah Christ. No-one really notices that the world turns and never stops turning. And that there are little creatures on it that all breathe in the same way the same air. The 'Melbourne Visitor's Guide' tells me that the original Kelly armour is on display at the national library so I ask a gaol guide for directions and he points to a tall tower in the sky and tells me to head for that but that it's closing very soon so

I dash round to that tower and check my bag in at security. It's in the 'Changing Faces of Victoria' exhibition, the armour, on Level 5 of this colossal, cavernous cathedral of a building. Lift. Up. Level 5, big glass case and there it is – Ned's original armour. The very one he wore, bullet-pocked, heavy-looking. It's missing the helmet, which is on a national tour, apparently, which is disappointing; there's always something you can't see, isn't there? Always something missing. But there are photographs here, too, taken during the final shoot-out; there's Ned himself, crouching behind a fallen tree in his steel suit, pistol raised. There's the post-office in flames. There are the gnarled and blackened corpses of Ned's gang, dragged from the smoking ruins. It takes a while for what I'm seeing to truly sink in; real photographs of Ned Kelly? Of the final shoot-out? *Real* photographs, from the time? The most primary of sources? Apparently so, yes. I wasn't aware such things existed. Why aren't these more widely known? Why haven't I seen them before? For three decades I've been interested in Ned Kelly, read the books, seen the films, visited the exhibitions, and this is the first time I've even been aware of the existence of these photographs. Who's been hiding them from me?

That afternoon, I meet with Fiona Gruber, a lovely, sweet woman, originally from Shropshire, who runs Melbourne City Radio. She interviews me in her house for her afternoon programme. I notice a book on her shelves: *Diary of a Welsh Swagman*. What's this? Something else I've never heard about. By Joseph Jenkins. Collated by William Evans. I make a note of it, and a mental note to search for it in every bookshop I'll find in Oz from here on in. It's her husband's book, Fiona tells me. His surname is Williams. Has an interest in Cymric things. I arrange to meet her later and Tony and I catch a cab to St Kilda. Once Melbourne's Kings Cross, now gentrified, a bit. I saw a play once, in Aberystwyth, called *St Kilda Tales*, about transvestism and drug use and madness and abandon and desperate celebration in the area, and I've wanted to visit the place ever since. So I drink in the Prince of Wales and the Espy, the Esplanade Hotel, which is brilliant, and allows you to smoke. The sky gets black outside. Stars bounce off the sea. Has this place got anything to do with the British St Kilda, I wonder, the remote and abandoned island off the coast of Scotland? I don't know. But it's a great place. Tony likes it, too.

Fiona comes to pick us up with her husband and they take us out for Chinese food. The next day we get back in the van and head for Adelaide, and our uncle, our mother's brother. The desert creeps ever closer.

THEN

They arrive in Adelaide at 2:30 in the afternoon and book into the Glenelg motel in what appears to be a posh part of the city, coastal resort kind of area. The clocks in South Australia have gone back an hour. Recently, there have been killings in Adelaide which have earned the city the soubriquet of 'Australia's Murder Capital'; the Beaumont children of '63 will never be found, and, some years later, there will be the Snow Town murders – people killed as part of a social security fraud, wrapped in plastic and stored in bank vaults. The killers will earn $800 from this crime. Luckily, the boy is unaware of these details; he's an imaginative child, given to anxious fretting about and dwelling on the world's lurking darkness.

On May 10th, they catch a tram into the city and feed ducks with bread. The boy asks whether they'll be going to see Uncle Roy. *No*, says his mother. *He's away*.

On May 11th, they leave Adelaide and head for Kimba, on the edge of the great desert. The pass through a hamlet called Iron Knob.

–A man built a robot here, the boy says. –A man robot. But it went wrong and there was an explosion and it blew up into hundreds of little bits and all they could find of it was its iron knob.

His brother and sister laugh. The mum writes in her diary: 'We have driven through some desolate places today and through miles and miles of nothing.'

Outside Kimba, they stop at a menagerie. There is an eagle in a cage, which seems to like the boy; it shuffles closer to him along its branch, cocks its huge head, makes clucking noises in its throat. There is a huge red kangaroo, taller than the adults, so tall it blocks out the sun. The chicken-wire of its enclosure bulges where it has leant back on its cable of a tail and kicked out with its hind legs. There is a fox skin drying on a wall, nailed to the wall. It is very hot and flies whine and cicadas provide a constant background shrillness. There is a crocodile too big for its pool. An American tourist wants his picture taken with the giant kangaroo so the zoo's owner lets him into the pen and the 'roo picks him up and bounces off with him. He's like a doll, the American, a small and screaming doll.

NOW

–So why couldn't we see Uncle Roy?

–It was Doreen, his first wife. Remember her? She didn't want us to visit.

–Why?

–Dunno. She was just like that. You remember what she was like.

I don't, really, but I remember the disappointment at not going to see Uncle Roy when we were in Adelaide, the mother's brother who lit out for Oz in 1966, the year I was born. I'd seen him since, in Britain, but we would see him again, in his adopted home city, at the other end of the Great Ocean Road, which is beautiful. We didn't drive this way as kids but we do now, and see the Twelve Apostles, huge towers of red rock rising up out of the surf far below, and we pass through small and attractive coastal towns, one of which, Kingston, is declared by a sign to be 'WINNER 2005 BEST MEDIUM-SIZED TOWN'. Bloody hell. That's scraping the barrel till it bleeds. At Mount Gambier we spot a Hungry Jack's, the burger joint in which I had my first ever experience of fast food, so we stop and go in. It's pink and yellow and garishly overlit. The soundtrack to *Grease* is on the jukebox, too loud. The food is utter shite. Cardboardy-greasy-meaty flat grey thing in a dry bun. Fries like blades of straw. Rubbish. All it does is fill a hole and make me feel slightly queasy. I don't often eat fast food, but I remember Hungry Jack's from when I was a kid. Was it this bad then? I remember liking it. Why did I like it? Has it gotten worse since I was a kid?

We get to Adelaide. The Glenelg motel is still there, same address, looks the same. Rooms for $69 a night. The pool, the low units. Hardly changed in thirty years. In the seventies, we caught the tram here, from Jetty Road, into the city. And we couldn't see Roy, then. But we do now. I give him a call and he arranges to meet us by a school so we get there and wait for a bit and there he is. Looks the same, too. He's been ill with cancer recently but he's recovering and for a seventy-five year-old, doesn't look at all bad. Hasn't aged much. Seems, sometimes, as if the only thing that's grown older is me.

Roy Mostyn, Ten Pound Pom. Was a policeman in Liverpool. He contacted the Oz police force for a transfer but they said he'd have to resign and then re-apply so that's what he did. He was thirty-two, a bit too old for the State Police, but the Commonwealth Police said yes, provided he went to Darwin. No skills were needed, really, just a medical and an interview; 'effortless', he says. He didn't really want to leave Britain, but followed his first wife to Oz – her siblings had emigrated and were loving their new lives. Roy remembers, though, looking over to Liverpool from New Brighton and seeing the city covered in a cold, grey smog; he was holding his daughter, Dawn, at the time, who was two years old, and it was that view that made up his mind to go. The boat journey took five weeks; 'best holiday I've ever had'. The irreversible fact of his re-location only really hit him when he'd bought a house and car in Oz, which left him with $15 in his bank account. Why Adelaide? Because his wife's sister was here. When he landed, it was raining, miserable, half ten at night. Arrival formalities at Outer Harbour, then herded onto a bus to the hostel. 1,800 people. The ship was full to capacity. Roy's first job was selling insurance, then he was a security officer, then he spent twenty years in the catering section of an Oz airline. He split up with his first wife, and married Eileen, a

Ten Pound Pom too. He refuses to take out Australian citizenship, or even dual citizenship, because he doesn't want to completely sever his ties with the UK. Does he feel Australian? 'No; I feel like a Pom. I'm proud of my heritage.' Which is of a piece with his innate loner nature. If he hadn't've met Eileen, he'd be in a little remote cottage in Wales, he says. There are greater career opportunities in Oz, it's got the best health system in the world (and he should know, having recently recovered from two primary cancers), money goes further, Oz war veterans are revered. Is there anything he misses? 'The friendliness of people', he says (he'd be shocked and disappointed, I reckon, at how rude Britain has become since he last visited, but I don't tell him that). Anti-Pom attitudes are very conspicuous in the workforce, he says, and talks about the overt aggression of the average Oz male.

And, nutshelled, that's my Uncle Roy. It's lovely to see him, and Eileen. We go for a pie-and-pea floater (a brilliant invention) and fish and chips which, of course, come without vinegar. I go to the supermarket next door to the chippy but all they have is raspberry vinegar. No malt. My God, what have these people got against vinegar? I'm considering wringing my socks out over my chips. We go to a 'pre-loved' bookshop in the city which doesn't have *The Diary of a Welsh Swagman* and while I'm in there the phone rings and the proprietor picks it up and listens for a moment and then says:

–Mate, you *so* don't understand what kind of a bookshop this is. Never ring this number again.

I wonder what was going on there? Wonder what he was asked for? We stay in Adelaide for two days then head out, north, into fairly featureless flatland, green shading into red, long straight roads to the horizon. Road trains; huge, monstrous things, three trailers long, you'd first see them as a dot miles away in front getting bigger and BIGGER and **BIGGER** and then they'd be on you with a massive blast of iron and backdraft that would set the van madly wobbling. Endless ribbons of tarmac ahead. A low bump is called Mount Remarkable, I think, but then we pass the low bump and I see the real Mount. Which is, yes, kind of remarkable.

The country starts to get emptier, harsher, hotter. Blasted, baked. Red sand. Scrub, desiccated. Leafless and scrawny trees.

Port Augusta. Pleasant, sleepy little town. Laid-back, relaxed air. High aboriginal population. We buy some supplies for the van; dried fruit and water and stuff. Leave. Into sudden, abrupt desert; red, endless desert. Quintessential Australia. Scrub and what grass there is a kind of bluey-grey colour, in sharp contrast to the red dust of the ground. Fine talcum. A dread desert, stretching ahead for a continent. Bit of apprehension creeps in. And now the sun roars in the sky. Flat blue of the sky. Vast and without mercy. I think of blistered, popping skin.

We're on the Nullarbor, now, its eastern edge. I've seen enough of deserts of both sand and ice to know that they're *not* barren, desolate places, and to believe so is to bow to a speciously inverted and unquestioningly received 'knowledge' that benefits only the aggressively colonialist mindset. Look closely, and listen to what their inhabitants – human and animal, vegetable and mineral – tell you and you'll realise that deserts are jumping with abundant life. Not just that; they're labyrinthine libraries of offered knowledge. But I'm daunted, to say the least, as the country's fierce interior opens up around me and I see ahead of me what I suddenly remember very, very clearly – approaching a distant crest in the road then going over it only to see another distant crest in the road and so on and so on and so on – and I'm filled with a deep admiration for what my mum and dad did, all those years ago, their bravery, three young children and another one on the way and all of them in a Holden car travelling across some of the emptiest, most hostile terrain on earth. Terra nullius. An extremely courageous thing to do.

–Tell yeh what, Tony says.

–What?

–I'm filling up with admiration for me Mum and Dad.

–I was just thinking the exact same thing.

An environment hostile to human life, unless, of course, that life has spent scores of millennia in the environment, patiently learning its moods and sensitivities, learning from it with painstaking care and attention. One lesson lasts centuries, spans generations. But for anyone else? Then this place can raise a red thumb and smudge a human life out against the blistered tarmac. Just more roadkill to be scavenged by the dingoes and crows and wedgies. Small bloody smears, not much bigger than the splats on our windshield.

I feel like a pioneer. Bit hungry, too; I feel like a pie in 'ere. Christ that's not funny.

The slagheap that rises blackly above Iron Knob is still there, but a lot bigger. Things have a tendency to shrink as you get older, but not this; the hill of muck and sludge is three times the size it was. It's now a range of hills in itself. Empty, empty place. We park up on the hard shoulder and get out and the silence hits me like the humidity did in Singapore; physically, and powerfully, like a hard slap across the face.

Kimba still has its motel. I remember the town, like something out of a western, wooden walkways raised and railings. Another Oz Deadwood, seemingly unchanged, except the menagerie's gone; the nice lady in the tourist information place tells us that it was in Cleve, south off the main highway. She remembers it; she's lived in Kimba over forty years. I'm disappointed. And amused, very, by the sculpture of the galah (Kimba promotes itself as 'The Home of the Big Galah'); a house-high pink model of a galah looking aloof and constipated. It's rubbish. Makes me laugh. Tony's in fits, drives around it in the van:

–Look at him there!

He can hardly drive for laughing. The van's rocking with it.

Kimba opens out into immeasurably vast wheatfields, horizon to horizon, endless. Wales would fit several times into these fields. It's a sea of green, young corn shoots, immense. Other cars pass us in the opposite direction, as they did thirty years ago, on the plain, and each driver salutes or raises a finger, just a small gesture of support and solidarity. Quite sweet, really. But evidently not for the police; we get pulled over for speeding just outside Minnipa. A big, fat, officious officer crooks his finger at Tony, who gets out to speak to him. I get out too, to lean against the hot bonnet and smoke and eavesdrop.

–What do ya do, back home?

–I'm a civil servant.

–Policeman?

–I *was*. Merseyside transport police.

I hear the unimpressed and utterly unmoved silence. Small 'zip' as a piece of paper is torn along a perforated edge. Then Tony's voice, incredulous:

–*Two hundred and seventy nine bucks?*

Aw Jesus. I'm all for not paying the bleeding thing – I mean, they're not going to chase us back to Wales – but my brother, he's been thinking that he might want to come back soon; his Sydney poledancer. And they won't let him in if there's a warrant out for him for non-payment of a fine. So what can I do? We're in this together. I suppose.

The sunsets have an intense beauty. They bounce redly off the leaves of roadside trees and look like a million fireflies. Such deep, glowing red. Past Wirrulla, we notice a car following us with its lights off. I think of *Wolf Creek*.

–It'll be another copper, Tony says. –That one who fined us will have radio'd on to his mate in Wirrulla and told him to watch out for two brother Poms in a Britz van. Bet yeh.

He overtakes, and sure enough, it's a police car. He puts his lights on as he passes. So that's not dangerous, driving at night-time with your lights off? For fuck's sakes. At the sides of Oz roads are raised plinths bearing the mangled remains of cars; warnings to drive safely. The coppers, evidently, take no notice of them.

Red desert darkening, stars coming out. Ceduna, which is now a metropolis compared to what it was, to what I remember it as being. My dad bought a boomerang here, or rather, swapped twenty cigarettes for it off an old aborigine in a pub. It's an amazing piece of work, decorated with intricate depictions of emus and 'roos. Which pub, I wonder? There are loads. And will the old aborigine still be around? I doubt it very much, judging by the state of the aborigines I see in Ceduna; they're desperate, people, drunk, filthy, fighting each other. They're heartbreaking to see. Facial features of natural nobility and strength, often now obliterated, robbed of all dignity and meaning by centuries of oppression, of conferred non-status. Forgotten as people by those who took from them everything that made them people. Hideous, this. I offer ten dollars to an old lady sitting on the pavement and she takes it without a word, can't even look up at my face. God, the shame in her. Coming off her in waves. I hope the money helps, in whatever way. Some time later, as I'm eating Chinese food, I hear a commotion outside the restaurant. There's the old lady, fighting with a younger man. She's screaming and scratching his face. He's kicking her. A waiter dashes outside to shoo them away.

We eat our noodles and ribs and get back in the van and drive on. Hypnotic, this – driving the desert in darkness. The world shrunk to two twin cones of light and the small slice of tarmac they illuminate. Trance. Trance.

THEN

Nullarbor Station to fill up on petrol. The car's covered in thick red dust, banks of dead insects in the grille and under the wipers, heat rising in a shimmer off the bonnet. The boy likes how it looks. He goes with his father into the shop to pay for the petrol and recognises the man's accent and his father and the man talk for what seems like hours. *What you doing here? Which part of Liverpool you from?* The boy gets bored. Outside, his mother honks the horn.

–One thing to watch out for, the man says, –on the desert. The abos, like. They'll come running out of the bush towards you, waving for help. What you won't know is, they'll have a spear between their toes, dragging it, like. So whatever you do don't stop for them.

And, indeed, a few miles before Ceduna, this happens; an aborigine with a wiry grey beard down to his belt buckle crashes out of the roadside bush, waving his arms. The children shout. Their father doesn't stop or even slow.

–He might be in trouble!

–And we might be 'n' all if we stop. Not taking the risk. You heard what that feller said back at the garage.

The boy thinks about this. Ambush. Spear. Robbery on the highway. He's been warned many times in Oz to look out for the 'abos' but he can't help but find them fascinating. They're so strange, to him. They have such kind faces. There'd been Afro-Caribbean kids at his school in Liverpool but they weren't like the black fellers here, in Oz. There's something intriguing about them, here. Back home, they were the same as him, just with a different skin. But here... he likes their voices. When they speak he likes their voices. And he sees them in Ceduna, lying in heaps on the pavements, sees his father exchange cigarettes for a boomerang and he finds the boomerang absolutely captivating. Loves the feel of it in his hand. It's a beautiful thing. The old feller who made it smiles toothlessly at the boy and gives him a wink and the boy is confused further. This bundle of stuff: Deception spear robbery ambush dirt drunkenness artistry no teeth friendly wink asleep in gutter kind faces nice voices watch out for the abos, boy. What's he supposed to do with such a tangle of information? All will come clear when he's older, he thinks. All will be explained, some time.

They leave Ceduna and head for Cocklebiddy, but before they reach that they see a motel at the side of the road – the Mundrabilla Motel. Look okay? Let's stay here. They do. Nice name, Cocklebiddy. Like an old shellfish.

NOW

We're looking for somewhere to park up for the night and sleep.
Somewhere off the Eyre Highway with its road-trains bellowing
past, somewhere away from the eyes of bored desert coppers
who might knock on the window and search the van just to make
their lives a wee bit less monotonous. I'm in a kind of trance.
Kind of asleep but with my eyes open. I open the road map on
my knees and shine a torch on it and look. A turn off just before
Nundroo will take us down to a wee place called Fowler's Bay,
right on the coast. Looks interesting. Let's go there.

–Wonder why it's called Fowler's Bay?

–Cos Robbie Fowler owns property here. As well as most of
Merseyside.

We turn off. Tarmac stops. Turns into dirt-track. '16 km', a
sign says. 16 km! Christ, it's a mere millimetre on the map. As if
we're a submarine wobbling through black ink, thick ink, the
dirt-track goes on. And on. Fowler's Bay itself is a few lights and
a sign on the outskirts saying 'NO CAMPING IN TOWNSHIP' so
we turn off and find a layby just behind the 'WELCOME' sign.
Park up. Climb into sleeping bags. Sleep. I wake at sunrise and
go out for a pee and *look* where I am – huge dunes to the left, a
vast bog to the right, a cold and whistling wind. I explore the
tiny village, walk out on the pier over the sea, watch the sun
rise. I see holiday flats advertised. A sign for a bar. For a caff,
too, but that's closed. Here I go again, thinking about spending a
winter in this place, huddled up against the storms that would
come crashing in off the sea. Looking out for whales.

I go back to the van.

We drive on. Just past Nundroo, we make a stop to look at
the dirt-track that's been running parallel with us since we

entered the desert and on which, as a family, we made the original journey, all those years ago. Tony can recall the tarmac road being built at the same time, on our right, then, as we drove down the track. For all those endless miles. I don't remember that, but the thought of doing this drive on that potholed and dusty interminable ribbon of a scrape in the desert floor... Jesus.

And we drive on. 'Nullarbor' is a Latin word meaning 'no trees', and up till now I'd thought it a misnomer; there are hundreds of trees. Thousands. Stunted and scrawny little things, yes, but trees nonetheless. Just before Nullarbor Station, however, the trees stop. Extremely suddenly, they stop. TreestreestreestreesNONE, like that. Flat expanse. We stop to take photographs. The sense of isolation almost overwhelms.

And we drive on.

THEN

The boy makes a moving world with his Action Man and books and pens and anything else that comes to hand that can be turned into a toy. He's aware that a vastness is going on outside the confines of the car but within the little moving box he creates his own world to explore and explore it he does, every cliff and cranny and coast and cataract and city and river and lake and heath and marsh. They sleep in motels, and, on occasion, in the car. One morning the boy wakes up amongst his slumbering family and, as quietly as he can, creeps out of the car. They've been sleeping in a car-park behind a motel or bar or something; 'NO VACANCIES' on the sign. It's hot, and still, and silent. The boy spies a long furry tail hanging out of a dustbin so he approaches the bin and lifts the lid and before the rising cloud of whining flies envelops his face he catches a glimpse of carnage, koalas and possums and wombats all stuffed into the bin, contorted, rotting, boiling mass of slimy fur and gnarled claws and milky-filmed eyes and seething maggots. He drops the lid and runs.

NOW

At the eastern end of the Bight, the great scoop that dents the country's southern coast, we see a hand-painted sign: 'COME AND SEE THE WHALES'. We follow the arrow, park up, pay our ten bucks each at the turnstile, move down towards the sea on the grid of wooden walkways that overhang it and my God, there they are, just below us, a group of southern right whales, adults and babies, huge things, lolling in the waves, hanging motionless in the blue. Incredible, beautiful, awesome. The largest weighing fifty tons, huge animals. Through the hired binoculars I see their great grins and callosities and flicking tails. I am completely thrilled. I am breathless. My skin sings. Such incredible, impossible animals. I've seen whales before, several times, and at closer quarters, but I'll never feel anything less than profound awe and wonder were I to see them every day of my life. Their sheer size. The way they play. And nothing prepares you for the sound of their blowing, the huge basso *roar* of it. And the smell of it, too.

We spend a couple of hours whale-gazing and even continue to squint at them through the binocs when they're little more than black smudges, way out to sea. And then we drive on. Always we drive on. Approaching Nullarbor Station, we see a young dingo at the side of the road, close by, unruffled, nuzzling the earth next to a sign that tells us not to feed the dingoes. The pub's still there, the pub where my dad met the scouse feller, but it's staffed entirely by Aussies, now. I wonder what happened to that man. If he's still in Oz, or if he's back in Liverpool. Another dingo is skulking around the pub and the petrol pumps. Pretty animals; like tall, white foxes.

THEN

It's spelled B-I-T-E, the boy thinks, because that's what it looks like, as if a colossal sea-creature has taken an almighty chomp out of the country's underside. He studies the map, traces the contours of the feature, sees that it's actually spelled B-I-G-H-T and concludes that the mapmakers couldn't spell.

They enter another timezone on May 13th. The clocks go back forty-five minutes. They stop in the desert as the cover has blown off the roof-rack, exposing their cases and trunks to the searing wind and the fine punk dust. Luckily, everything stayed on, held down by the guy-ropes; losing the jerry cans of water would've been calamitous. The boy thinks of that, of thirst, of what it'd be like to die from dehydration. How it would feel, in the indifferent desert. He can't imagine it. Can't comprehend any kind of death.

They're on the dirt-track for six hours. Jostling, bumping, rocking six hours of choking dust and heat. The children must cling to the seatbacks or the door-handles, anything they can, for six hours. They see two foxes and an eagle and stop to photograph the eagle which, when developed, will show a speck on a bright blue background. When they stop, the ground feels unsteady and strange under the boy's feet, like it did when he stepped off the plane back in Brisbane. He's tired of this journey, now. He wants it to be over, wants to be in Perth.

NOW

Christ but this is getting boring. Pure monotony. Flat and featureless and seemingly endless. Stultifyingly dull. God how it goes on. No settlements between Nullarbor Station and Eucla, and a brief glimpse of the sea on my left is about as exciting as it gets. And Tony's singing Roy Orbison's 'Crying' for the fourth time. Every word of it, from 'I was alright' to the closing 'OOOOH'. I'm going fucking mad. The landscape's beginning to pound, pound me down. I can't stop yawning. I've been getting intermittent twinges in my left leg for the past few hours, due, probably, to the unrelieved cramped conditions in the van's cabin, and I start looking forwards, with genuine excitement, to the next one. *Anything* to break this flatness, *anything*. It's crushing, this journey. Indescribably dull. And it never ends. Flatness, smoothness, on and on and on. Please, God, bring me a hill, a hummock, a bend in the road, anything to relieve this nothing world. What if I've died and gone to hell? What if this is my punishment, to travel this featureless road for all eternity?

There are no land predators in Australia, apart from the salt-water crocodiles in the north, and they don't stray far from the water's edge anyway. Plenty of harmful spiders and snakes, of course, but they don't want to eat you; they're not going to stalk you or ambush you or regard you in the way that you might regard a roast potato. Whereas in the Namib, or the Sahara, where I was hunted by a leopard and looked into the face of a lion with nothing between our eyes but two feet of scorched air, in those places where I was nothing but a morsel for cats the size of cows, I felt all my aspirations and sense of who I am fall away, the position of myself on the planet was tattooed onto my soul and I felt a kind of religious awe and terror which grew quickly into something like an ecstasy, a sort of low-level but constant rapture, which settled in me and never quite left. Being awoken at night-time by the sound of roaring lions or the snorting and stamping of rhinos or the whooping of hyenas, knowing that, to many of the other living things around me I was nothing but meat, this, I feel, puts a wonder in the heart. It adds to the constant joy of discovery. You're a child again, with the golden, murderous gaze of a lioness on you. Without such animals, such predators, however, the desert eventually becomes just a chore. It rapidly loses whatever magic it may have had; it's just heat and dust and no shade or water, no respite, no joy. The Namib filled me with the awe of connectedness. The Nullarbor just pisses me off. I hate being bored. I want to be stalked; want all of my senses to atavistically and defensively sharpen and hone and clarify themselves. Want a huge and ferocious and spotted cat to see the van as a can of Spam.

The checkpoint at the border of Western Australia comes as a huge relief. Something to do, something else to see other than the horizon-to-horizon sheet of unbroken one-colour emptiness. This checkpoint wasn't here in the seventies, but I'm glad of it now. Breaks the tedium, a little. It's manned by very pleasant border guards, both with matching hairstyles and goatees. Maybe that's a requirement. We have to give up all our fresh food, but we can keep the dried and canned. I eat some apricots and we get waved through, into WA, which is exactly the same as SA. Oh look! More treeless plain! For fuck's sake.

THEN

Leaving the cafeteria of another motel after another huge breakfast of eggs and steak and toast and jam, the boy's father gently touches the mother's stomach and remarks that she's putting on a lot of weight.

It's all these big breakfasts, she says.

They exchange a look which the boy can't read.

Further. They drive further. Into Eucla, on the state border. Here, in a layby, is a sign, the EYRE HIGHWAY sign, which tells the boy's family that they're roughly halfway across the Nullarbor. To the left is PERTH 895 MILES, and to the right ADELAIDE 809 MILES. Nearly 900 miles to go, still. From Liverpool to the Shetland Islands, or even further. The boy can't really grasp these distances. They're a slice of forever, to him. His world has become the moving car and motel rooms glimpsed for a night and his world to come will be the same thing. The journey has no end; the journey itself is the end. There is no destination but this constant forward movement.

NOW

It's the same sign, look. Believe that? The exact same sign.

And it is, exactly the same, the only difference being that the distances are now given in kilometres, not miles. Thirty years of weathering have bleached the colours and cracked crazily the lamination and scaled the iron struts with rust but it's the same sign. I'm amazed at this. All those years, through all that growing, this sign has stood here, waiting for the boy that once gazed at it to return as a man and gaze at it again.

Through all personal mutability and development and slipperiness and general dream-like insubstantiality, through sadness at the mortality of things, through fear at the inexorable tread of time and melancholic anxiety at the undeniable trend of people and things to change and veer and become quite else, through all of that, this sign has remained a constant, on the other side of the planet, waiting to tell me how far I've come and how far I've got to go. I'm halfway through the journey. Everything else has changed, but this sign has stayed the same. Thirty years. Almost a poet's lifetime. Through war and heartbreak and weddings and funerals and everything else. I find this absolutely amazing and as I photograph it I realise my face is split in a grin. I'm halfway through the journey, the sign says.

The long running road out of Eucla, and the view of it from the top of the hill, both my brother and I remember it, clearly; it, too, is now as it was then. This place has hardly changed at all; the units of the Motor Hotel are the same ones that we slept in as children, the hotel's sign is the same, the shop. Time has passed this area by. It remains untouched. It just stands still as the world whirls around it. My expectations – that I'd feel old on this trip, in a place like this, sadly remote from the child I was – are confounded here; I don't feel a great distance from that boy at all. He's me. I'm him. I've just sprouted from him. The acorn's in the oak. It's not like he's standing next to me or anything like that, he's just simply here. There's a kind of comfort in this realisation; a peace, even. I feel something settling down inside.

And we drive on. The endless road, parts of which bear strange markings on the tarmac; they double up as airstrips, for flying doctors and other airborne emergency services. It goes on. Every judder of the van begins to bang in my head. My ribs ache. The cabin becomes a fetid moving coffin. Rancid pie-gas leaks out of us both. I read the roadsigns; the next large settlement after Eucla is Norseman, 712 km away. Seven fucking hundred and fucking twelve fucking kilo-fucking-metres. The Nullarbor map and guide that I've brought with me tells that Norseman, once a gold-mining town, is so called because a prospector named Laurie Sinclair tethered his horse called Hardy Norseman to a tree overnight sometime in the 1890s and by morning his pawing hooves had unearthed a big nugget of gold. Since then, 'over five million ounces of gold have been taken out of Norseman'. The town contains, apparently, the Beacon Hill Lookout and Walk Trail, the Tin Camels and the Statue of Norseman, the Dundas Coach Road Heritage Trail, gemstone fossicking (sigh) opportunities by the ancient Dundas Rocks and Bromus Dam picnic area, and a Tourist Centre where you can get your Nullarbor Crossing certificate.

We pass a garage and an adjoining motel.

–When will we reach Norseman?

–That was it.

It just goes on. Madness starts to cling to the radiator grille. How did my parents manage this journey? In a car, with three screaming childen and an unknown fourth on the way? I'm hungry I'm tired I need a poo mum tell him. Needing food and water, sleep, looking after? God knows. I'm barely keeping it together myself. I let the boy in me entertain himself, construct tunes out of the rolling rhythm of the van, absorb the passing landscape. It just goes on.

THEN

Madura. The car's overheating. Steam hisses from the bonnet and the gauge is right in the red.

–Dad, stop! We might blow up!

They pull into a garage and the children jump out and run across the forecourt, away from the huge fireball that the car is about to turn into. A mechanic looks under the bonnet and fiddles about for a bit and removes something.

–It's ya thermostat, mate. All blocked up. I'll fit another one for ya.

He does, and the car cools down. The mother's leg pains get worse. They stop at Cocklebiddy, where there are, apparently, interesting cave systems, but a sign warns of many dangers so they don't explore. The Baxter Cliffs are nearby, too, but it's getting dark so they drive on to Caiguna and sleep there in the car. The dad looks for this place on the road atlas and cannot find it. *Some of these places aren't even on the map,* he says, and the boy wonders if they really exist.

NOW

As if in sympathetic memory, my legs start to hurt, being cramped in the same position for hours at a time in the van. I worry about deep vein thrombosis. You hear of people getting DVT on the flight to Australia but not whilst in a van driving across the bleeding place. They ache, my legs. Quite badly. I rotate my ankles to boost the circulation but that does no good at all.

Madura. Great views over the Roe Plains from Madura, which was settled in 1876 as a horse-breeding station for the

British army in India. Christ, and the colonisers disdained the aborigines for being nomadic and unsettled? How blind and self-deluded is it possible to be? And outside Madura, on the plains, my God look! There's a bend in the road! We start going up a little bit of a hill! I don't know if I can stand the excitement.

I'm getting hysterical. We pass a sign for the 'EYRE BIRD OBSERVATORY' which has two crows sitting on it, and I'm delighted to see that. Bird observatory. Two crows looking. Signs for the Baxter Cliffs and Caves which once more we bypass, but I consult my guide and discover that John Baxter was the overseer for the pioneer Edward John Eyre and 'tragically lost his life on 29 April 1841', although it doesn't say how, nor why his death was more tragic than anyone else's. We plan to spend the night in Caiguna, sleeping in the vehicle as we did as kids, but when we park up and unroll our sleeping bags we decide that we're not tired so we drive on, straight into the fresh hell of the 90 Mile Straight, 'the longest straight stretch of highway in Australia', ninety unrelieved miles, straight as a ruler, unbroken, a new depth of tedium. Trance. Trance. Just what you see in the headlights, that's what the world has shrivelled to. Tarmac. Yellow light. Drone of the engine. At the end of this straight is Balladonia, where we'll be off the plain, but that's a world away. My brain shuts down, hardened by boredom like my arteries are by too many pies eaten quickly at garages. Trance. Trance. Drone. Drone. No thought but a big white block of air. Drone.

The horizon still lit a little by the rays of the setting sun. Shafts and sheets of lilac light shot through it like swathes of violet rain. Trance. Drone.

Did I find this journey as soul-crushingly boring all those years ago as I do now? Was it like wearing a suit of armour then as it is now, stifling and airless, a weight on my flesh, an unpleasant almost physical presence in my skull? Probably not, no; I was a child then, nothing was boring, smells and sounds and tastes were awaiting discovery. I couldn't imagine, then, what true boredom was like, how it is one of the worst insults that the world can dump on you; how even pain is preferable to it. Left to my own devices, I'm never bored, and rarely was as a child, until school and then work began their bleaching and bludgeoning. But what can we do, on the Eyre Highway's 90 Mile Straight, but drive? Drive and drive and drive? Drone, drone. It never ends. I will never leave this road. I never have, in fact; I'm still on it. I never left it as a child. I'll still be on it when I'm old and doddery. Let it end. Please let it end.

THEN

–What's that on the road?

They squint through the dusty windscreen and, outside that, the dusty air, at three thin figures on the road ahead. The dad slows the car to a crawl and slowly approaches the figures which materialise, out of the heat shimmer and swirling dust-clouds, into emus, three emus crossing the road. The family gawp. The boy is agog. The birds walk with a peculiar gait, their feet delicate and high-stepping but their necks and heads slowly bowing and lifting. These are birds; like sparrows and crows and parakeets, these things are birds. What wings they have are folded behind their backs and their feathers more like shaggy fur. Impossible animals. Pillows on legs. Pillows with long necks. Something prehistoric in them, in their scutellated feet and tiny eyes, something that could only have come from the ancient red sand and the sharp orange peaks of rock and the trees festooned with streamers of shed bark like sloughed skin. The boy has grown used to seeing mirages on the road ahead, images of water, and he wonders if these birds might be of a similar phenomenon. He can't take his eyes off them. They have knees and ankles, and like starlings and seagulls they are birds. He wonders where they are going. Wonders what purpose draws them to whatever particular place they are aimed at in the colossal continent he's almost traversed.

NOW

If I was outside, alone in the desert, with a pack and a tent, I'm sure I'd feel differently about it; I'd be more attuned to its smells and noises, more open to sensual stimulus, feeling its vast hostility like a throb in the blood. Its lack of land predators would, I think, mean that I'd grow tired of the place quite quickly, in comparison, say, to the Namib, but my experience of the Nullarbor would be an intense and exciting one, at least for a time. As it is, though, in the cabin of the van, confined, hot, bored, and tired, I just want the fucking thing to end. It's nothing but a big beach, and without the sea. It's shite. I want to be in Perth.

–We're in Norseman, Tony says.
–What?
–We're in Norseman. Just saw a sign.
–Thought we'd already been through Norseman?
–So did I.
–So that means we've still got one fuck of a way to go?
–Looks like it.

–Ah Christ.

Roadkill, a lot of roadkill; 'roos and wombats and wallabies, on their backs, bloated, front paws spread as if in surrender to the seared sky. Sometimes, as we pass, huge eagles rise up from these carcasses, flapping massive wings in what looks like a monumental application of will, lifting their great bodies up beyond the cones of the headlights into the outer darkness, ribbons of rotten and dripping flesh trailing from their clenched talons. It's a mad world, out there. We don't see any emus, either alive or dead, but we see plenty of these huge raptors; disturb many a frenzied and festering feast.

Drone, drone. Trance, trance. Drone. On and on and on.

We're tired, now. We pull into a layby beyond Norseman and unroll our sleeping bags. According to the map, we're now off the plain. The desert is behind us. We've crossed the Nullarbor, for the second time in our lives. I feel nothing but a tiny celebratory jolt in the stomach and then I'm asleep.

THEN

Kalgoorlie and Coolgardie. Adjacent townships, but an Australian adjacency, which means many miles in between. Ex-mining towns, quiet and ghostly, like old towns in movie westerns. The boy imagines having a shoot-out in the main street, and being shot; this often happens in his mental fantasies – he's often the loser, the one who comes off worst, but he delivers a stirring and moving speech at the point of death, supine on the dusty street, his precious life-blood spilling out, attended by weeping women and devastated admirers.

They stop for a while in Kalgoorlie and visit the mining

museum. The boy buys a tiny model wheelbarrow made out of what looks like lolly-ice sticks, with a nugget of nickel on it and a small chunk of quartz which bears a tiny fleck of gold, real gold, a wee twist of dazzling colour. He's proud of this purchase, the boy. He keeps it for decades. He owns some real gold.

His mother makes an entry in her diary: 'Kalgoorlie is a sad place with so much to tell and no-one there anymore.'

Back in the car, their father shows the children a page of the road atlas. Points to where they are, and then, a few inches away, to Perth.

–See? We're on the same page.

–Will we get there today, dad?

–Might do. Let's see.

They move on again. Again they move on. The boy holds his wheelbarrow in his hands and gazes at it.

NOW

Like Ceduna, and several other towns, Kalgoorlie is a metropolis compared to what it was in the seventies. It's lively, and busy, and gives the impression of always having been so. I'm surprised. The Federal Hotel advertises 'SKIMPY OF THE WEEK' on its noticeboard, which is cut to the shape of a naked woman. 'Skimpy'? What does that mean? A bikini-wearing contest or something? It's Sunday morning, so much of the town is closed, but the place has that air of hiatus that busy towns on Sundays always give off. Apparently, the mineral industry in WA – nickel, mostly – is booming, and mining towns such as this one have been re-populated and re-energised. Mansions on the approach roads declare much money. There's an airport. Several pubs and restaurants, and many caffs, all busy with breakfasting and brunching folk, in one of which we order juice and coffee and eggs from a German waitress. Tony wolfs his then goes off in search of an internet connection. I order more coffee and have a read of the Sunday papers. Main news concerns the problems of child and domestic abuse in the aboriginal communities; booze and hard-core pornography are to be banned from the townships for six months in an effort to prevent this abuse. Policemen are to reside in the reserves to enforce this embargo. I read utterly harrowing stories of rape and neglect and addiction (one young guy, arrested several times for child abuse, says that he needs to drown out the screaming in his head by making others scream loud enough for him not to hear it). These are a people in despair. I've seen it worldwide; in Arctic Inuits, in native Canadians, even in Celts at home. It never loses its power to perturb, in whatever landscape it takes place. Here, letters to the papers insist that the current measures of prohibition are either patronising or are simply too little, too late; indigenous voices offer opinions as to how to remedy peculiarly aboriginal ills, and others declare that we shouldn't heed indigenous voices simply because they're indigenous (well, maybe, but when have aboriginal opinions *ever* been listened to?). An aboriginal novelist writes a fascinating article which applies cultural murder to individual lives, illustrating the horrifyingly actual and tangible human damage inflicted by institutionalised racism and disen-franchisement, and then states that self-respect must come from within; she directly addresses her people and tells them that no-one else can confer self-esteem upon them. It must come from within; within the communities, within the tribes, and within the breast. I find myself nodding at this, but then stop myself; it's too easy for me to agree, here.

But dignity. Dignity is innate, *not* conferred, it is as much a characteristic of the human animal as is walking upright, but it *can* be forcibly removed. The drunken blackfellas in the gutters of these small and isolated towns, they're like that not because they naturally lack a sense of dignity or self-respect but because they've had those qualities systematically and ruthlessly and mercilessly taken away from them, over centuries. A human being stripped of dignity and sense of self-worth is easy to ignore and brutalise (as, indeed, is an entire landscape; mining companies etc. back home work on this principle). The western suburbs of Sydney have similar problems, but they have access to all the grog and wank-mags they can afford, and why? Because they're not aboriginal. So the ocker in his flip-flops and singlet in the Federal Hotel, drooling over the latest weekly skimpy through the last tepid and spittled inch of his tenth Toohey's, feels superior to the blackfellas brawling and puking in the car-park outside because he believes that he has an innate dignity which the other man doesn't. Of course self-respect has to come from within, but so does respect for others, and in a society like Australia's, where institutionalised bigotry has its corrupt counterpart in many an individual marrow, I don't see that happening. Not for generations, at least.

Tony comes back. We talk about spending a day and a night in Kalgoorlie but then decide to press on to Perth. Let's get it done. Perth's 590 km away. So we drive on, again, through Coolgardie, which is as I remember Kalgoorlie as being, thirty years ago, empty and windswept and deserted and surrounded by red desert and ragged scrubby patchy bush. Beyond it, the desert continues. Even the trees are now red. This is a landscape evolved to repel the human, it seems – all jagged and arid and spiked and comfortless. Except humans lived in it, quite happily, for 40,000 years.

And still it goes on, the journey. Straight roads to the horizon, then another straight road to the horizon. This landscape pummels you, batters you. It is without mercy or respite. Outside Southern Cross, a sign directs us to the 'SONS OF GWALIA GOLDEN LEAD MINE', but we don't go. Just want to get to Perth.

THEN

It's become a kind of dream, a dream of perpetual forward motion and the monotone sound of the car's engine a never-stopping drone in which the boy has started to discern rhythms and voices, a peculiar music. This car is his home. In his fuzzy trance he has noticed that the passing landscape has changed and there are now houses and civic structures and green-ness and tarmac roads, other traffic around. Indeed, the car close in front hits a wallaby; the animal springs from the bush on the left, the car clips it, it rolls over a few times and ejects a long straight squirt of silver piss into the air then leaps up onto its hind legs and disappears into the bush again, on the right. The boy knows that the sight of that will be burned into his mind for ever; the helpless animal, the fountain of pee, the sudden shock. The expression on the wallaby's face.

The father turns round in his seat. –You okay?

The children nod. Ask questions about the wallaby; will it die, where's it gone, is it hurt. The father reassures them and continues to drive and night starts to fall and they enter Perth at 6 p.m.

NOW

A large part of the culture, it seems, is concerned with visual warnings; mangled cars raised on plinths at roadsides, sometimes in elevated cages, to remind drivers that 'SPEED KILLS'; pictures of diseased gums and fat-clogged arteries to remind the smoker that 'NICOTINE KILLS', not just on packets of cigarettes and tobacco but on billboards too, huge memento mori for the addict. No, note, images of cirrhotic livers or glassed-open faces to illustrate the dangers of alcohol; no drowned blue lips to warn against surfing; no compound fractures to dissuade you from rock-climbing. (The human animal will always seek danger. If it harms no-one else, then let it happen. Just let it happen.) These images are of a piece with the surface, depthless beauty of much of Australia. And anyway, the cause of death is birth; might as well have a billboard image of a pregnant woman squatting over an open grave and be done with it. 'BIRTH KILLS'. Yes it does.

We pass the Merredin Pioneer Village and I remember, at one such place, feeding a wild bearded dragon with Opal Fruits. I'd been taken there on a school trip and snuck away from the group into the bushes and made friends with the big lizard. Was it this one here, at Merredin? Can't recall, but the look of it doesn't set any bells ringing. And this is Sunday, so it's closed. But I do recall, clearly and in detail, the little dinosaur, his scales and teeth and eyes. How his wild proximity thrilled me to my heart.

The land gets drier and harder as we approach Perth. Baked dead. It must've been a long and harsh summer, and in fact the roadsides are flanked by signs exhorting us to 'SAVE EVERY DROP'. At a garage we buy Chico Rolls and the taste of them whooshes me back thirty years in time and I buy a Cornjack too and put it up on the dash while I go to put some garbage in the bin. As I'm out of the van, Tony takes a bite out of the Cornjack and puts it back in its wrapper, upside-down. Laughs his head off when I get to the bottom. He's regressing back to his thirteen-year-old self. Turning back into the wicky get he once was.

A dream this has become. A kind of dream. This country is vast and I move at the same constant speed through a landscape that never changes so it's like I'm not moving at all yet time and distance pass. It's like floating. Like being a figment of someone else's dream. The noise of the engine and the slipstream of air begin to seem like they're hiding voices, and all of this is motion back towards the younger me. The years are slipping away yet at the same time I'm feeling every one of the thirty years between the then-me and the now-me. Feel every broken and healed bone, the ripped beginnings of every scar, the deleterious effects of every cigarette I've ever smoked and every drug I've ever drunk or snorted or injected. Every sleepless night. Every panic attack. Every moment of sadness. Every time my heart has been stabbed in rejection or bereavement. Every dead pet. All of this, I know, will soon transmute itself into joyous surprise at survival, and the happy appreciation of the accretion of experience. Just got to wait for that to happen. I know it will, though.

The village of Meckering promotes itself as Australia's 'Earthquake Centre'. Better not stop there, then.

The ground greens, swells into hills. This must've been promising to my parents, after so many days on the baked and treeless plain. I seem to remember it; the tree-lined road on the gradual decline. This long gentle slope into Perth, this is what I remember. This is where the car in front of us hit the wallaby. The silver urine. Dark clouds gather above and that's a good sign; in WA, rain is welcomed, has been prayed for. The approach road has been widened and re-surfaced and generally improved, probably several times over, since I was here last, but the feel and camber of it are unchanged. I'm remembering it, quite clearly. Rain falls, now. In a suburb, we pass a Chinese take-away called The Ming. Better not stop there either.

The damp greenness is a shock after so much flat aridity, and soon, in the dusk, we see the distant city, from high up on the road. Oz cities, from a distance, look impressive, futuristic; tall and sparkling. Like Brisbane, Perth looks much, much bigger than I remember it as being, but I don't, at the moment, feel that intrepid excitement that I usually feel when I approach unfamiliar cities, perhaps because, even if it *is* at thirty years' remove, I'm re-discovering this one. I've been here before. It was home for two years. A sense of returning home isn't entirely absent, now, but what I *don't* feel, oddly, is a wave of relief at arriving, at the journey being over, at the end of the plain's battering monotony. Thought I'd be whooping in rapturous relief and glee but I'm not. I'm just tired.

But the writer-brain, or the survivor-brain (which might be the same thing), kicks in, and through the fog of exhaustion and boredom I start to wonder how I'll describe the Nullarbor crossing, in written words. How to make that hellish trek readable? Is it possible to write such a journey in an exciting and interesting and compelling way? No, my inner voice says, slow and droney, like a 78 r.p.m. record played at 33 and a third: I'll go for literal transcription. I'll go for mimesis, and make it as dull and frustrating to read as it was to actually do. Sod the reader's comfort and fun: Share the misery. Make it a chore, a task, onerous, to read. Drag the reader into the gaseous and stifling cabin of the van, on the endless red desert. Make them suffer, as you did. Share the misery.

Now there's relief. *Now* there's a lifting of tension and tautness from the shoulder muscles and neck and the gut. I feel some peculiarity of shape on my face and realise that it might just be a smile. Ho ho. Here we go. Welcome to Oz.

We pass a sign for Welshpool and traverse Griffiths Street. The globe shrinks. It's 5:10 p.m. when we enter Perth proper, for the second time in our lives, on June 24th, 2007.

PERTH

THEN

They stay in the Swan View Motel, not far from the River Swan,
hence the name, and sleep deeply. The boy, when he wakes, has
become physically accustomed to the world being still again –
he's not reeling when he stands – but when he looks out of the
window he expects to see it whooshing past and is momentarily
surprised that it isn't. The next day, the family visits the Migrant
Services Unit in Perth city centre. They see Mr Myatt, who
makes some enquiries about a Migrant Transit flat, and a man
called Bruce Aldersley who advises the boy's parents to
'remember that you've got no money'. He gives a small wink as
he says this to the boy's father who, outside, calls him 'a Good
Man'. The boy can hear the capital letters in his dad's tone. It's
like being an immigrant again, except he's travelled overland this
time, not through the air. And departed from the same country.

They are quickly allocated a flat, in Robertson Court, in the district of Yokine. The children make friends very quickly, the boy with, amongst others, a Northern Irish boy whose father had fled to Oz to escape the IRA who were seeking to punish him for some transgression. One day the Irish boy cuts his hand open and bleeds heavily and talks about the time his dad pushed the IRA man through a window and opened an artery in the man's leg. He tells this tale in a very low voice. This particular friendship doesn't last long; the two boys fall out and fight. The boy plays spin-the-bottle with a Scottish girl his age called Jackie Thompson and he kisses her and he'll never forget the glorious and squirming shock of her tongue in his mouth. He trespasses onto a garden to look at the fish in the pond there and the house owners see him and call the police who take him home and have a word with his parents and the boy is very upset, largely at the revelation of how pettily proprietorial some people can be. He just wanted to look at the fish. This might, too, be the moment when the sight and smell of uniforms sets up in him an automatic recoil reaction which will never leave him. The boy enjoys gazing into the inverted cones of ant-lions' nests, watching for the tumbling ant and the small eruption and the snapping jaws. Such miniature horrors there are here. As everywhere. The boy befriends a group of Yorkshire children, one of whom, Graham, likes to eat paper; when his elder sister tells him to stop doing this, he replies: 'Sumtahms ah eats it and sumtahms ah dorn't', which tickles the boy. He laughs.

NOW

I remember this – I remember the parks by the river, and walking through them, sitting on their grass, watching the parakeets, eating icecream. The city itself seems immeasurably more massive, but I recall little bits of it. Tony asks me what I'm remembering and I tell him about the parks and he tells me that he remembers punching me in the nose in one of them.

–I don't remember that.

–I sat on your chest and punched you full in the face. You ran away screaming and covered in blood.

–I must've blocked that out. What a horrible fucking thing to do!

I'm outraged, all over again.

–I was a little bastard.

–So was I, but I was never a bleedin' bully!

–What else are little brothers for, other than to punch in the face when you're kids?

Which is a point, I suppose.

We've travelled 6,508 km. We look for the Swan View Motel but it's not there, and there seems to be a much posher establishment in its place. We go in, ask at reception if anyone remembers the Swan View. Young feller asks the older members of staff but they shake their heads.

–Long gone, mate.

–Thought it might be.

I ask him for the tariff of his hotel and he quotes a huge sum. Bollox to that. Anywhere cheaper?

–In Perth? Nah. Yer best bet's Free-o.

–Free-o?

–Fremantle. Few miles to the south, ey?

Free-o it is, then. We get back in the van and drive again, only ten minutes or so to Fremantle. I'm exhausted. The town is very busy. All parking spaces are on meters so I mind the van while Tony runs into the nearby Irish pub to ask if they have any spare rooms. Shower, I'm thinking; bed. Proper bed. Scour the desert dust away and sleep like I haven't slept in months.

I'm leaning against the van smoking when a young feller approaches, early twenties, mixed race aborigine by the looks. Smartly dressed, but goes into a spiel about needing money, so I give him a handful of change and then Tony's there, squaring up to him, asking him what's going on.

–Bit broke, mate, he says. –Need a few cents.

–No you don't, Tony says. –Fuck off and take your mate with you from round the back of the van.

I watch, shocked and disappointed, as the feller skulks away, joined by his mate who'd been lurking behind the van, waiting to pounce. Gave that bastard about four bucks as well.

–Did you not see him? Tony asks.

–I didn't, no. Just gave his mate a handful of change. Pair of fuckers.

–Best watch ourselves around here.

Big brothers – they *can* be useful. Especially ones that have been in the marines and know how to spot an ambush. Yet each mugging I've narrowly averted, and there have been several, makes me angry; did those pricks think I look easily muggable? Do I look like I'll just surrender and give them my cash and wallet without a fight? I'm insulted. Feel like running after that pair of wankers, daring them to try and roll me. If I wasn't so tired I'd do exactly that. In this state, tho, they'd have my pockets empty in a blink.

The Irish pub has a couple of rooms, so we park the van and I feed the meter a week's wages, and we take our rucksacks up to reception, check in, get to our rooms, unpack. A tiny room, just a bed and a wardrobe and a wall-mounted small TV. Good enough. All I need. Two shared showers, one of which is free, so I dive in it and wash slabs of accrued muck off my body and feel like I'm being re-born and go back to my room and lie on the bed and turn the TV on. I can hear pub hubbub below, music and laughter, smell the rising fumes of beer. Quickly decide not to go down there, tonight. The great plain's still in me. I just sleep.

THEN

Robertson Court is a brown building, arranged in a block-capital C, around a patch of green with a playground on it and some washing lines. Three storeys high. Stairwells and walkways. Each flat is high-ceilinged, with a sitting room and three bedrooms and a kitchen, all fairly large and basically furnished. It's an immigrant hostel, much like Yungaba in Brisbane, but physically different; it's less tropical here, cooler, less humid, more like a British suburb. There are small shady courtyards, perfect for playing football in and for examining the redbacks that make nests between the bricks. The children drop small pieces of debris in the webs to entice the spiders out; at the first glimpse of that bright red hourglass they run away screaming.

The family has very little money. On May 18th they go out looking for a second-hand TV but are unsuccessful; every seller, on hearing the family speak, seems to suddenly remember that they've promised their TV to a mate. Work is freely available, however, and the father shortly secures a job and a $100 sub from the boss. They buy a TV. Returning from the local shop one day, the dad gets talking to another occupant of the Court. The dad says that they left Brisbane because it's a 'hicktown' and the man yells 'so's Perth!'; in his Lancastrian accent it comes out as 'Puth!'. The boy is given the shopping to take upstairs to the flat and told to be careful because it contains eggs. 'So don't bounce 'em', says the man.

They drive out into a suburb to visit friends, Gina and George, who have four children, all girls. The adults discuss house-buying business and schools and the children eat crisps and watch TV. The girl who is the same age as the boy, in her night-dress, lies on her tummy to watch TV, head propped up on her hands, and the boy discovers that, in a certain position, he can see her bare bum. So he stays in that position for so long that he gets cramp in the entire left-hand side of his body.

NOW

Don't bounce 'em. Odd, the trivialities that we remember. Why should that comment have remained in my head? I remember the bloke who made it, too, what he looked like; quite rosy face, greyish-sandy curly hair. I remember that he was wearing faded blue overalls. *Don't bounce 'em.* Very strange, the details you retain.

Higgy's flying into Perth to meet us in a day or so, to ferry us around, at which point we'll be returning the van, so we scoot around Perth in it, do a wee bit of revisiting. Tuart Hill School is a low redbrick building, still there, not much different from how I remember it. It's play-time (or 'recess', as they call it here), and hundreds of kids are running about in a playful panic, so I can't take any photos. Can't point a camera at kids who aren't related to you, these days. Thirty years ago, I was one of these children. Running about and shouting. That was me.

We drive out to Yokine. Robertson Court is now private accommodation, with a locked security gate, so we can't enter the grounds. Discuss climbing over them but decide against it; images of Oz security guards Hitlerised by their uniforms. And relishing every last second. A sign outside reads: 'WHY RENT? IF SIZE MATTERS, THEN THIS IS IT!' How much did the copywriter get paid to come up with that meaningless twaddle? The flats *were* big, though, as I recall; voices echoed in the rooms. I had my first proper kiss here. On that balcony, there. With Jackie Thompson. Wonder what she's doing now? We can see the window of the lounge of our old flat. The storm-drains are still there; whole worlds to intently and intrepidly explore, they were. The nearby row of shops used to have a chippy where we'd buy sausage and chips and take them home to watch *Dad's Army*, behind that window, there, on the corner of the nearest building. Me. Three decades ago. *Dad's Army*. Chips and sausages. Did Oz chippies have vinegar then? Spin-the-bottle. The ant lions. The redbacks. Can't remember about the vinegar. Thirty years. Jackie Thompson's tongue. A torrent, an avalanche. *Don't bounce 'em*.

THEN

The immigrant children amuse themselves by telling the Australian children fanciful stories about Britain. They tell them about scouse mines, porridge mines, open-cast cawl mines, about stalking haggis in the glens. The boy had done this in Brisbane, too, but here, he begins to entertain and entrance himself by creating fancies of another sort, on paper; in Perth he begins to write, he doesn't know why, only that an untouchable part of himself is demanding that he does so. He can contain the world, when he's writing about it. The world seems less brutal and merciless, seems to make more sense, when he's writing about it. Writing thrills him, makes him feel truly and madly alive, gives his presence on the planet a point. The world's riches are available to him when he's writing. In later life, he will achieve similar states of ecstasy in sex and drugs and snorkelling and standing atop mountains or travelling fast in cars or encountering wild animals, but it'll stay with him always, this initial thrill, this first contact with one of the beauties of being alive. His reading consists largely of horror stories, and he is obsessed with films of rampaging animals – *Jaws* and *Grizzly* and the like – and his writing reflects that; one of his books is about a pack of mutant wolves devouring the world. He shares this passion with another boy, David, who also writes, and who, one evening on a Court balcony, insists on reading out the first few pages of his novel. He stands and solemnly declaims the first line: 'The great snake stood lying there'. Our boy bursts out laughing. Not cruelly; he just can't help himself. There's another boy, too, a boaster and liar who has been everywhere, done everything. One evening he bores and annoys the boy by ticking off all the many swimming certificates he's achieved, so the boy asks if he's won his Swimso badge yet. *Ah yeh – got that one when I was eight.* Our boy laughs and dances and points. *No you didn't! It doesn't exist! I made it up!*

The boy's sister, with her friends, has a money-making idea: they'll knock on doors and dance to Abba songs for money. On their first night, they make a few dollars, but it's all American. Every last cent.

Work is so freely available that the father can effectively try several sites before he chooses the one that suits him best. Most of his co-workers are surly, miserable, taciturn, but he does find one good workmate, an Italian, whose name – Antonio Indicalatto – fascinates the boy; he mutters it to himself, under his breath, relishing its rhythm, marvelling at its music.

On May 25th, at 10 a.m., they gather around the TV to watch the Ali fight. That afternoon they go into the city and the boy is bought some *Jaws* pumps; ankle-high boots with a jagged sole like spiky teeth and a picture of the shark on the side. He loves them and wears them until they're falling apart on his feet. His mother has a friend, Marge, who she secretly calls 'Marge the Moaner'. They often meet mid-morning for tea and a whinge.

Life, to the boy, is both exciting and worrying. He's settling into, and is starting to cease fighting against, his nature; his idea of the world made up of equal parts wonder and disgust. He's beginning to accept. He loves scrumping pomegranates, and scouring the undergrowth for insects and animals, and watching the strange and musical birds in the bushes and trees. He is terrified and sickened by the bullying he witnesses, and by the images of the war in Vietnam he still sees daily on the television. He's growing. On the way home from school one day he walks past a driveway to a big house. The driveway is carpeted in bits of pretty green stone and he and his friends stuff handfuls of it into their pockets and bags and, the following weekend, take it to a jeweller's in the city. The jeweller's assistant, a young woman, examines a piece of the stone and says 'you could be rich, y'know'. Outside, the boy does a little dance of joy. When they return later, the jeweller himself has had a look at the stone and he tells them: 'It's false jade. You got it off someone's driveway, didn't you? I'll give you $2.48 for the lot.'

They visit Kings Park. There is a memorial wall, listing the names of Australia's war dead, and the boy's mother looks for 'Griffiths', something the boy will do for the rest of his life. There's a slice taken out of a tree, huge, tractor-wheel-sized, with tags on it marking historical events; when the tree was the width of a saucer, Australia was founded as a colony; a vinyl LP, World War One broke out, and so on. The boy is entranced by this, rapt; human history accruing as the tree grew, still and alive at the world's heart, an unknowing chronicler of a vast and never-ending story. And the rings in the wood, the concentric rings, they draw the boy's eye and mind in toward the centre, from sapling to seed, hundreds of years before he was born. When the wood and the world was waiting for him.

NOW

There are great views over the city from Kings Park, the Swan River pushing its own silver through the skyscrapers. It reminds me of the Memorial Park in Washington DC, commemorative monuments everywhere you look. A young country making its heroes, its legends. This is a very different Perth to the Perth of the seventies. Almost unrecognisable. I find the Memorial Wall, and again search for the 'Griffiths' name. Still none. I look for, and fail to find, the tree-slice, so I go into the Information Centre and speak to a lady there. Tell her that I'm returning after thirty years and what I'm looking for.

–The section of tree? she says.

I'm startled. –How the hell did you know that?

She laughs. There's a funny twinkle in her eye. Psychic, she must be. She tells me that the wood was rotting, infested with white ants; the park authorities repaired and treated it on several occasions but it eventually became irreparable, so they fed it into a chipper and spread it over the park. 'So it's still here in spirit', she says, and laughs again. I like this lady.

Outside, I point my camera at the floors of flower-beds and take some pictures of woodchips. There's a small and dry mat of them beneath a tree and I sit on it; the chips are soft and comfortable. I take some sandwiches and the *Guardian Weekly* out of my rucksack. Glasgow airport in flames. Blair gone, replaced by Brown. The world goes on happening. Look where I am.

I wander through the park, amongst the monuments. There's Queen Victoria, surrounded by cannons; the two dated 1843 were used in the Crimean War, and those dated 1813 and 1814 at Waterloo. There's a floral clock. A cenotaph; 7,000 names from the First World War, 4,000 from the Second. So much slaughter. A Jewish memorial. Shells from the HMS *Queen Elizabeth*, presented to the park in 1921 from the ship that gave covering fire to the Anzac soldiers at Gallipoli in 1915. And there's a memorial to the victims of the Bali bomb in October 2002.

I drift through the Botanic Gardens. Remember, vaguely, visiting here with the school, although I'm not entirely sure about that. Certain events we remember vividly, others through a fog of uncertainty, and the clarity of our recollections has nothing to do with the importance of the incident. And we remember things that might not have happened at all. But the flowers look and smell nice. And when I sit down outside the caff with a can of Tango I discover that I have woodchips stuck to my arse.

THEN

Life leaps from event to event. Exploring the edge of a field one day, not far from a digging farmer, the boy and his friends chase a scorpion under a rotting log. They roll the log over and reveal a brown coil of a sleeping snake; the boy grabs its tail, holds it dangling out at arm's length, laughs and shouts. *Look what I've found! Look what I've got everybody!* The farmer roars, runs, whacks the sleepy snake out of the boy's hand and decapitates it with a shovel. Turns a furious face at the boy.

–Stupid little *ber*-stard! A taipan! Lucky it was hibernating! What are ya doing waving bladdy taipans abaht? Stupid *ber*stard!

The boy's shocked and upset. The farmer, not an unkind man (except to venomous snakes), puts his big hand on the boy's shoulder and tells him of the dangers of handling snakes.

–You've got to be careful here, son. Yer not in Pommie-land now. Snakes here'll bladdy well kill yer. That taipan? One bite and...

He snaps his fingers.

–*Deadly* poisonous, son.

Out of the side of his eye, the boy can discern the writhing death-throes of the headless snake, brown loops of it rising above the tops of the long grass then sinking again. He will not look too closely. The killing of the snake has upset him about as much as his own close escape. Not that it feels like he's *had* a close escape... all he's aware of is that he's just witnessed the killing of a wild animal.

The mother announces her pregnancy to the children. *You're going to have a little brother or sister.* Her diary at this point is full of crying. It mentions a lot of rain, too.

They visit Rottnest Island, primarily to see the quokkas,

small mammals like kangaroos the size of rabbits, but they see none and, in fact, memories of visiting this island will fade quickly. The boy must've found it unexciting, and even when he returns to it thirty years on he will remember very little about it.

The boy likes the TV series *The Six Million Dollar Man* and watches it avidly. The only times he does not rush in to watch it is when he's out kissing Jackie Thompson.

The boy's teacher at school is called Mrs Lamont. They don't think highly of each other. She writes in one of the boy's reports that he wanders aimlessly around the classroom and will often simply walk away when she is talking to him. He 'drifts', she says, meaning both mentally and physically. He takes his revenge by introducing a character called Lee Mont into the book he is writing about a man-eating thresher shark. This character is attacked and eaten whilst diving on a reef. The shark devours him from the feet up, and when it reaches his torso, jets of blood pump from his snorkel. The boy is proud of this detail.

He makes friends with an aborigine girl. Two outsiders together. Thirty years later, the man the boy will become will wish, very much, that he could remember this girl's name as clearly as he remembers her face.

The school he attends is called Tuart Hill. On the first day, the boy's sister's teacher is attacked by magpies; she has bright blonde hair and walks under the tree in which the birds are nesting. After that, she has to wrap a towel around her head whenever she walks to and from her car; evidently the magpies are angered by the colour of her hair. The boy finds this intriguing. In the playground one break-time, the boy watches ants dismember a redback spider and drag it down into their nest in a crack between two paving slabs. The spider's bulbous body will not fit but the ants pull and pull until it bursts and issues a greenish fluid. The boy feels sick but cannot look away. Two older girls stop by him and say in a sarcastic tone: *Oh, veeeerry interesting*. The boy remains squatting. Their bare brown feet are close to his face. He feels a bit foolish, but remains enthralled by the ants. He sees the girls' feet. He's enthralled by them, too, feet, ants, feet, ants. He looks from one to the other.

The mother works in the school's tuckshop. She sells small salty crackers pasted in either jam or Vegemite for one cent each. The boy often buys twenty; ten Vegemite, ten jam. Eats them all and feels queasy, but again buys twenty the next day.

The brother befriends a fat boy, Shane, who never wears shoes and who has a glass eye. He often skips school, this boy, preferring instead to sniff petrol with another barefoot boy, Bruce. The brother is disturbed by this, as is our boy when he is told about it. Sniffing petrol. What happens when you sniff petrol? How does that make you feel? Nicer than normal?

At this point, the family has been in Australia a little over a year. A year. Two Christmases. It feels like a lifetime.

The brother steals foreign coins from a classroom, and buries them at the base of a tree in the school grounds. At assembly the following day, the headmaster announces that they've been found. *There's a thief in our midst*, he says. *Someone must know who he is*. The boy suppresses a chortle.

They visit Yanchep National Park and the crystal caves. There is a chip shop in Yanchep village overlooking the sea at which they often eat, but sometimes they will make use of the barbecue facilities in the park. One day, at a picnic bench, the father is about to bite into a sausage when a kookaburra swoops and snatches it from his fork, an inch before his face.

Uproar and hilarity. The family is delighted by this. There are swimming pools in Yanchep and the boy comes to them with his school. Fighting a fear of water, he dresses up in a snorkel, mask, flippers, rubber ring and armbands before he enters the pool. But he eventually beats his fear. Drowning wasps sting him. The family goes out on the park's lake on a rowing boat to watch the turtles swim beneath them.

Trig Beach, where the children snorkel in the rock pools. Quinn's Rocks, where they walk or spend a day, sprinting barefoot and yelping across the sun-scalded tarmac of the car park.

The brother joins a boxing club, and in 1976 wins a trophy. He never forgets the name of his opponent: Conrad Frankie. The boy watches the fight from a front-row seat and finds it thrilling. Thinks that maybe one day he, too, would like to box. Some distant point in the future.

Wanneroo Lion Park. They have their photograph taken holding a baby lion.

At the top of each page of the mother's diary is a motivational phrase, and the one for September 15th – three days after the boy's tenth birthday – reads 'work conquers all'. This will blink back into his memory in a decade's time when he starts to read about the Second World War and Europe under Nazi occupation. Work conquers all. So said Australia, in 1976.

In October there's an eclipse of the sun. The boy is taught how to make a pinhole camera at school, but most parents keep their children indoors. If you're told that you absolutely must not look at the sun, the ten-year-old you will look at it. So the parents keep their children indoors, all curtains closed.

Jets fly over the city, one dusk. One pilot, as he roars up into the sky, leaves his after-burners on. Thousands of people as one gasp.

Accumulation of sight and sound and taste and touch. A life is made then measured in a million drips and drops.

NOW

8 Elizabeth Road, in Wanneroo, still stands. More – it's barely changed. I have a photograph if it, thirty years old, but it could've been taken yesterday, so unchanged is the house. The facade is exactly the same. I'm amazed. A man's working in the garden. Me and Tony and Higgy approach him and show him the photograph, tell him what we're doing, our reasons for being there, etc. He looks at the picture and it's his turn to be amazed. He's from New Zealand. His name's Toby McAnally. He invites us in to look around but asks us to excuse the mess: 'she'll clear it up later, when she comes back from work', he says.

Ah, our enlightened antipodean friends. No wonder Germaine Greer left. Although I wish that she'd go back, to be honest.

The back garden has been changed, has been raised and patioed, although the black boy bush is still there under which we buried a cat after he'd been run over. His bones'll still be there, maybe. On the night he died, he leapt up onto the outside windowsill of my bedroom and pressed himself against the mosquito screen. I close my eyes and see his tabby fur sticking through the mesh and then I go down the side recess of the garden to stand at that window. I once slept behind there. In that room, there. And my cat once stood on that ledge. Cat long gone. Me still here. Kind of. Toby tells us that he bought the house a few years ago off an English couple who'd let it 'go to rack and ruin'; he had to take seventeen trailer-loads of garbage out of the back garden. We look inside. There's the cupboard and laundry room in which two of our other cats had kittens. Tiny, weeny kittens. One of the cats developed mastitis so my mum had to feed the kittens out of a bottle. I was entranced by them. There's a brass cockatoo on the wall in precisely the same place where we kept a real cockatoo, Georgie, an incessant screecher of a bird. There's the arch in which my sister, Nicola, as a baby, would entertain herself, and us, in her suspended bouncy chair. She'd cackle uproariously as she bounced, for hours on end. I picture her there, as a tiny baby. Picture the kittens in the hallway, all of them scampering as one back into the cupboard when something startled them. Picture all of us younger, much younger, mum and dad, brother, sisters, myself, in this room, watching telly, doing jigsaws, playing games.

We leave. The patch of bushland at the end of the road, that's still there, too. It used to contain a half-burnt out tree with a hollow in its trunk in which we made a den and in which I stayed for a couple of days after reading a book called *My Side of the Mountain* (author long forgotten), about a boy who runs away into the American wilderness. I got sick after eating half-raw sausages cooked in the old aborigine way – wrapped in eucalyptus leaves and buried beneath a fire – and had a tick bury itself in my leg. I remember gouging it out, twisting it, ripping it out; it left a scar, a small purple blotch like a birthmark, that I have to this day. There was a pond in this bit of bush, too, at which I once thought I'd caught a glimpse of a platypus, but some of the scrub has been built on now and I can't find the pond. And I imagine that the tree has fallen and rotted away.

I'm feeling a mite peculiar. The house looked exactly the

same. The bush didn't, but it nevertheless pushed back into me the sense of pure and tangled adventure in which I seemed to mostly live, those days. Of course we age. We get old and we die. But how many of us regress like this, to the other side of the planet, to revisit ourselves at a distance of three decades and 12,000 miles? My head's what, I don't know, no; the feeling's not in my head, it's in my lungs. Creeping up into the pipes of my face.

We drive to the school. Higgy's borrowed a car from the daughter of his sister, and her husband, Tommy, a lilac girly car with 'Hot Shot' written on the side. Three burly blokes inside it. What does he think we look like? I'm laughing. I put my bush-hat on and tie a bandanna around my neck just to look a little gayer. Think about buying a bushy fake moustache. We drive out to the old school and I go into reception where a nice lady, after I've explained to her what I'm doing there, tells me to come back later, after the kids have gone, which is understandable. The leathery green leaves of the plants, the prehistoric-looking ferns. I'm seeing these things again. The long sloping hill that leads up to the school; I remember my grandfather walking up that hill in the intense heat, dripping with sweat, carrying a bag full of ice-cold Coke to meet us after school.

I go to Wanneroo shops. There's the hairdressers where Tony got his ear pierced. There used to be steps here with two thin parallel ramps up them for pushchairs; I would ride at them full pelt on my bike, shoot off them at the top. Only a few inches wide, these ramps, and steep, so, if your aim wasn't perfect and speed not enough, you'd smash into the steps. They've been concreted over, now. The butcher's shop at their crest is now a Cole's supermarket. I went to that butcher's with my grandad, who gave the butcher far too much of the unfamilar money; I corrected him, and the butcher told my grandad not to bring me with him, next time.

The supermarket where I won $1 on a scratchcard is still there. I bought an item for 99c and told the checkout lady to keep the change. I was punched in the nose outside these shops; I'd been winding a bigger boy up all day, throwing spiky seed-pods at him, poking fun. So he punched me. I bled profusely. He later turned up at my parent's house, on his own, to offer an apology, after which he became a mate. Seems like I was punched in the nose a lot in Oz.

We drive out to Mullaloo Groyne, a spit of land that used to be linked to the mainland by a bridge, but has now been turned into an isthmus. We would fish from the groyne, watch the seals and porpoises swimming beneath the bridge. Tony caught a catfish, which stung him. We'd catch rock cod, fearsome things with giant jagged teeth; the first time Nick Macleod reeled one in, he screamed and dropped his rod. The arrangement of the rocks is exactly the same as it was. Contours, shapes, all as I recall. The abutting beach used to be a carpark with a shack which sold icecream. We'd run to it yelping over the hot sand and tarmac. Now there's a green sward with trees and a basketball court and a surf club and a caff at which we eat Moroccan-spiced chicken burgers on a terrace overlooking the sea and drink Kilkenny beer. The waitress is Irish. Look where I am. Look what I am, and what I'm doing.

Back to the school. I return to reception, re-meet the lady I met earlier. First thing I do is ask her if she has any record of a Mrs Finkelstein. She checks and says no. Is there any way I can track her down? Again, no. Probably not. I think about ringing all the Finkelsteins in the phone directory. I'd *love* to see her again. Let her know how important she was to my development. I'll never forget Mrs Finkelstein. Before this trip, I'd entertained thoughts of meeting her, buying her a meal, telling her that she made such an impression on the ten-year-old me that the forty-year-old me has travelled the planet just to tell her so. I've longed, always, to tell her so. I've never forgotten her. But it seems like I won't be able to do that; seems like she'll be impossible to track down. She'll be in her late fifties now, early sixties. Might not want to be disturbed, even if I could find her. Might be dead. In my memory she'll always be the way she was when I was ten.

The school is as I remember it, more or less. The assembly point was a square of tarmac beneath a roof, no walls, but now it's enclosed and has a stage. I sit on that stage. The headmaster once gave the entire school detention, I can't remember why, and we all had to sit under the roof until he allowed us to go. I absolutely hated it, but I did find a load of coins in the sand at the edge of the tarmac, which I surreptitiously pocketed. I remember the kangaroo, too, the huge kangaroo, bounding across the playing fields one lunch-time; the teachers screaming at the pupils to get inside, the panic and frantic delight, the huge and leaping beast. Parrots here, today, in the bushes and the trees. My classroom used to be split in two by a concertina divide, but now those two rooms are just one. It smells the same as it did. I breathe deeply in. What is that smell? Glue and carpet and whatever else. School-smell. Smell of the me I was.

There's a row of stainless steel sinks attached to the outside of the classroom. The same sinks, unreplaced. How welcome they were on baking days. I bend at one and take a drink. A gap of three decades between two drinks of water.

Driving away from the school, down the coast road back

into the city, a sadness creeps into me. No, it doesn't creep – it blunders. It's clumsy and abrupt and undeniable. I start to miss the younger me and mourn the death of him and mourn the gone years and I think of my grandfather, dead twenty years, and I think of Mrs Finkelstein and inexplicably I miss her with a sharp and sudden pain. Can you miss someone that you haven't seen for thirty years? How? And I realise that I'm missing my girlfriend and I'm missing Wales and I'm missing my home and I feel very, very far away from where I want to be. I'm in the back of a lilac car on the Wanneroo Road into Perth and I'm full of yearning and empty holes. My grandfather; his laugh sounds in my ears. Mrs Finkelstein; the expression on her face when she saw what I was doing to the blowfly and the terrible sensation of my plummeting heart. I want to be home. On the other side of the planet, that's where I long to be.

I will get drunk tonight, I think. I will drink to dead things, things that rot inside me and the world beyond my flesh, or of not rotting only then also resting under rich soil and pretty flowers and never to re-awaken in the forms in which I loved them, still love them. That's how I feel, suddenly, on the northern outskirts of what is often referred to as the most isolated city on earth. Given that, and the fact that this place was once my home a long time ago, then I should've really found the correlative to my mood; if I was going to feel at home anywhere, at this moment, in this mood, then it should be here. But it isn't. I feel abandoned and estranged within this skin.

We stop at Trig Beach. I go down to the rocks on the foreshore and sit on them and they look the same as they did all those years ago and the waves come in just the same, too. I find myself looking, outlandishly, for signs of familiarity concerning memory; for footprints of the younger me in the sand, for a sandcastle I might've made over a quarter of a century ago. As if the waves haven't erased every final trace. I smoke a cigarette and bury the butt deep in the wet sand, so it'll remain there longer, but that too has probably gone out to sea by the time I'm back in the car. Futile gesture anyway.

I don't hear the words that I speak on the short journey back to Fremantle. I know I'm talking, but I don't quite grasp what I'm saying. Back in my room at Rosie O'Grady's pub I have a shower and then walk around the town; a second-hand bookshop has some of my books on its shelves, dog-eared and well-thumbed, evidently read several times over. I should be pleased by this. I speak to the girl and she tells me that that writer's books are popular; his novels bounce off and back to the shelves regularly. I should be pleased by this. I return to Rosie O'Grady's and start to drink. Higgy and Tony pick me up, we drive out to Higgy's sister's house, where she and Tommy have cooked a huge and superb roast dinner. After weeks of pies and clingfilmed sarnies, this food is heavenly. The wine goes down quickly and in great quantities. There's me, Higgy, his brother Jimmy, Tom, Tom Jr, Higgy's sister Maggie, Tony, and a feller called Phil. I remember how, as a child, I would observe British people in Oz trying to export their culture, which meant full turkey dinners on a sweltering Christmas Day. And pud and custard. In forty-four degree heat. Ridiculous, But this food is now working very well on me and I'm necking wine by the bottle. We talk about Wales; Phil, a young Englishman, asks if I've ever been to Caldy Island. Not since I was a kid, I say. He tells me about the huge funfair there, the Ferris wheel and dodgems. Tony and I laugh.

–That's *Barry* Island, yer dozy bastard! Caldey Island's a monastery!

154

Hilarity. I picture monks on the waltzers. Dressed in their habits carrying goldfish in plastic bags.

I sleep in the van, outside on the drive, in the drunken stupor I had every intention of reaching, after Wanneroo, the school, Trig Beach, everything. When I wake, I lie there for a while, wrapped in my sleeping-bag, waiting for some indication of how I feel. Still sad? I don't know. I'm just alive. Hungover and alive. I get out and go into the house.

THEN

On December 17th, they move into a new house – 8 Elizabeth Road, in the suburb of Wanneroo. There begins to tickle and scratch inside the boy a thing which, in later years and after it has grown, adults will refer to as a 'feistiness', or a 'delinquency'. He likes pulling wheelies on his Oddball bike. He gets into fights, during one of which he has his nose bloodied at the local shops. Another he arranges with a boy called Neil Bennett, in the gardens of the council offices after school; they desultorily shove each other for a bit as other boys watch and then just wander away from each other. A fried chicken franchise is opened in the shopping centre. The boy loves the food from there. He always will, even after he discovers how bad, verging on the poisonous, it is.

The father's father visits and the children are overjoyed. They adore their grandfather (the mother's father died ten days before the eldest child, Tony, was born). He takes them fishing to Mullaloo Groyne; such creatures they dredge from the sea. The catfish, the rock cod. Some men who they don't know catch a small shark and cut it open and a baby shark falls out;

our boy doesn't witness this, but is told about it by his brother, and is deeply upset. It haunts his dreams. At the groyne they buy a dead barracuda off another fisherman and take it back to the boy's mother who shrieks when she sees it. One day, Tony casts and a gull takes the bait in mid-air. Frantic flapping and squawking and awful gurgling. The grandfather reels it in and slowly and gently releases the hook and the bird flies away.

They have friends, Gary and Darren. Their father is called Roger, and is from Corby, their mother is Scottish and part-albino. They have a swimming pool in their garden. Gary catches a scorpion and nails it to a plank of wood and ants eat its insides. The boy studies the ants, marvels at how he can see them moving like little scurrying ghosts inside the eaten-out carapace.

The boy also has a new sister. She is tiny. She's born on January 26th, which is Australia Day, 1977, at Subiako King Edward Hospital. 6 lb 4 oz. She is doted on. A photograph is taken; the grandfather, the dad, the children, the baby Nicola. All these generations so many thousands of miles away from their home excepting the newest, whose home is here. This is where she enters the world.

School: The boy is in Goolelal House. He does quite well at the subjects he likes, and atrociously in those he doesn't. He wins awards; a merit award for 'outstanding creative work in reading', the wording of which puzzles him even then, although the irony probably passes him by. The certificate is stamped with an angelic choirboy being blessed. Another award is given to him because 'his brain has worked overtime to achieve well in: Contract 54 points!' The accompanying drawing here is an odd one of a Dennis the Menace type character looking mischievous. What was 'Contract'? 'Inspiration' is a set task of a morning; the pupils are given a small blank booklet and asked to fill it with a story or essay or poem or whatever on a given theme. Marks are given out of three. The boy almost always attains full marks. He likes his teacher. She is called Mrs Finkelstein, she is young, pretty, and given to wearing, in the intense heat, white gossamer dresses which, in a sunbeam, opaquely reveal her underwear and bodily curves. The boy likes looking at her. He's aware that he regards her in a very different way to that in which he regards, say, the dinner-ladies, but he doesn't know why or what this means, only that when he looks at Mrs Finkelstein he feels a peculiar fluttering sensation somewhere inside his lower body. He looks at her a lot. Sometimes he finds himself inventing questions just so he can approach her desk and ask her and stand close to her and converse with her and smell her and make her smile. He's also, like the other children, the boys especially, reached an age where he's exploring notions of power; to this end, many children keep pet blowflies. They'll catch a drowsy blowfly and tie some cotton around its thorax and make of it a flying pet, tethered, on a cotton leash. When they grow bored they pull the knot tight and the fly falls in half. One day, the boy grows infatuated with his power over the blowflies and he pulls the wings off one and, as it scampers across his desk, tries to stab it with a compass. Absorbed in doing this, he is shocked to hear a gasp above him and he looks up and sees Mrs Finkelstein and in that instant he knows he'll never forget the expression on her face. *I'm very disappointed in you*, she says. *That's sadistic. And if you don't know what that means, go and look it up. I thought better of you.* She crushes the crippled fly in a tissue and throws it in the bin and the boy, his face burning with shame, goes over to the little reference library corner and takes down a dictionary and flicks to the S section. Looks up 'sadistic'. Reads: 'the gaining of pleasure, sometimes sexual, from the suffering of others'. There is a furnace in his face. His heart, wet and heavy like mud, plunges into his feet. That she should think that of him. That she should see that in him. The shame is utter. He'll never forget those words, this moment, her expression. Yet from such moments we grow and learn, and it is at this moment that the boy begins to become the man who will revisit this room thirty years later. From this moment on, the boy will understand the need to protect the vulnerable and the weak and to execrate the bully. There are times to come when he will fail in this, of course, and make mistakes, and, for a multitude of reasons, become for an instant a bully himself, but he'll forever recall the fly and the shame and Mrs Finkelstein's expression and the sensations of self-loathing which set his face and breast ablaze and that will be enough to steer and guide him away from the darker rewards of influence. This is all to come. Here, now, he tries to make amends with his teacher by being an exceptionally good pupil for her, by writing stories that entertain her and by looking after the weaker members of the class, and he makes amends with himself by surrendering to his wonder at nature and by becoming a member of the Western Australia Gould League, whose membership card reads:

GOULD LEAGUE PLEDGE
'I promise I will protect all birds,
other animals and plants, except
those that are harmful, and I will not
collect birds' eggs.'

Certificate of Membership
for 1977
Awarded to N Griffiths
C.F.H. Jenkins, M.A., President
Mrs. F. Sparkes, Secretary

He'll keep this card forever. The organisation has a code, too, to which members must pledge to adhere, and which reads:

THE GOULD LEAGUER'S CODE
(a) I will learn and keep all wildlife protection laws.
(b) I will keep the Gould League Promise.
(c) I will not pick wild flowers except for study purposes.
(d) I will not destroy trees or plants unnecessarily.
(e) I will do my best at all times to prevent bushfires.
(f) I will obey the rules for the keeping of pets.
(g) I will leave the bush as tidy as I found it.

The last point puzzles him a bit; the bush he knows, the patch of it at the end of his road, could never be described as 'tidy'. It is chaotic and crazed and that's why he likes it. It contains a burnt out tree with a hollow in its trunk against which he leans branches to make a den, in which he sleeps for a couple of days after reading a book called *My Side of the Mountain*, about a boy who runs away from home into the American wilderness and survives by building his own shelter and growing his own food etc. The fictional boy adopts a raccoon as a pet; the real boy adopts a grasshopper, which whirs away from him the first time he opens the matchbox. The fictional boy survives, at first, on hedgerow and woodland salads; the real boy eats a flower and has to spend a day in the school sickbay, throwing up (the headmaster is very amused at the boy's declaration that he thought the flower was 'quite edible'). The fictional boy roasts a trap-caught possum over a fire; our boy cooks some sausages in the aboriginal way, eats them half-raw and, again, is violently sick. When he's found, the fictional boy is healthy, muscular, almost a man; the real boy, when he returns home to his worried-sick parents, is dirty, bedraggled, upset, stippled with ticks and crusted in crap and vomit. But he thinks he spotted a platypus in the billabong in the bush and a big part of him remains pleased with that, above all else.

Other animals: Georgie, the cockatoo, given to the family by the Macleod family because it was too noisy. After a couple of weeks, the Griffithses give the bird to someone else, their ears ringing. TC the cat, who gets run over, and which they bury tearfully beneath the black boy bush in the garden. Two other cats, Bonnie and Clyde, which both have kittens in a Liverpool sports-bag in the laundry room, one of them accidentally killing two of her babies and developing mastitis, so the remaining kittens have to be put on the other cat, who rejects them, so the boy's mother then has to feed them by hand, from a minuscule bottle. The boy adores the kittens. His favourite is an all-black one which he calls Midnight. He's upset when they have to go to the pet-shop.

He catches a cane-toad and keeps it in a box under his bed. A highly dangerous animal, bright red fiery belly. His mother flips understandably out when she finds it. Tony puts a rubber snake in the parents' bed. The children huddle together in the room next door, giggling, waiting for the screams.

They find a huge spider in the garden, span of a spread hand. It's made a nest in a hole in the ground. The boy gingerly puts a twig into that hole and can feel the spider attacking it; the stick's movement vibrates up his arm like a shock-wave. And a bobtail lizard, a large, squat thing with a triangular head and blue tongue and pronounced scutellation which the cats are intrigued by. The children make an enclosure for it, which of course it escapes from, after a couple of days. *I knew it was going to run away*, Tony says. *It gave me a sly look this morning.*

And parrots and wasps and flying ants and locusts and wallabies in the bush and a hundred other wonders. Blowflies, too; the boy tries to make amends with blowflies. He makes a deliberate effort to regard them as wonderful things, and one day he studies one, buzzing angrily against the windowpane. He looks closely at its jointed legs, the compound eyes, the exquisite lacework of its wings. As he watches, it falls on its back and begins to thrash madly. He's about to catch it and let it out when, from where he imagines its arsehole to be, a worm begins to emerge; a long, white worm, filament-thin, a hideously wriggling thread which keeps coming and coming until it's three times as long as the fly itself and still it squirms out, writhing, the fly buzzing and spinning in what seems to be enormous distress and the worm twists and coils and uncoils and grows longer and thinner and the boy, his skull bulging with horror, picks up a heavy book and drops it onto the vile mess and then runs to the bathroom to be, once again, sick. Another lesson learned. Effective, if harsh, teachers, blowflies are.

NOW

We're talking about Georgie on the way to Yanchep. The incessant screeches he made.

–You ever had a cockatoo, Higgy?, I ask. –I bet you have.

–Get fucked.

Laughter.

Yanchep is big in my memory. It was the name of a national park and an attached village. I'd go there a lot, with the family and the school, swim, go out onto the lake in a rowing-boat. In the village, there was a chippy run by a British couple. Again, I think of the importation of food to a tropical climate from a climate in which that food was used as a kind of internal radiator. Is this daft or endearing? Neither, really; what it was was uncomfortable.

We drive out to Yanchep, north from Perth city. Outside Wanneroo, for miles, there used to be just bush, but now it's built on – long low estates which my dad would've worked on, had we stayed. Perth is expanding exponentially. In contrast, Yanchep Sun City hasn't changed much, from what I remember, but then I don't really remember a great deal about it; the approach road to the place is just an approach road, then and now. It's a seaside village. There are dunes. Some construction is going on amongst the dunes. The chippy at the Two Rocks Shopping Centre has gone so we eat pies instead. I ask for ketchup and the guy gives me a little plastic box of the stuff, matchbox-sized, in two conjoined halves. No lid, just the plastic box. I'm baffled by it. The guy takes it from me, holds it between his thumb and index finger, and squeezes; it snaps in the middle and releases the sauce onto the pie. What an unnecessarily complicated way to get ketchup.

–You wouldn't believe the amount of accidents with these things, the guy says. –If you were a Yank I wouldn't't've helped ya.

I laugh and take my pie outside. Oz pies are great pies, even though the amount of them I eat will boost my lipid levels hugely and unhealthily. But they're everywhere; so many different varieties all over the place, and each one tasting great. I'm surprised that Australia isn't a particularly obese or heart-diseased nation. If you've a weakness for pies, and a propensity to weight-gain, don't go to Australia. Or wear blinkers if you do. Or come fitted with a gastric band.

The shopping centre is as I remember it; the same beige breezeblocks, the blue sea in front, the same small harbour. I remember looking out over that harbour, sitting at one of these tables, eating fish and chips in the baking heat with my family. Yanchep National Park itself is, too, very familiar. There's the lake on which we'd go out on a rowing-boat to watch the turtles beneath us. Is that the same bench my dad sat on when the kookaburra swooped down and nicked the sausage off his fork? The *exact* same bench? Surely not. But it does look familiar. Tony recognises the tree under which we'd sit and picnic. Did I use the word 'picnic' as a verb, then? I hope I didn't. I'm slightly embarrassed about using it as one now. There's a koala compound, which wasn't there then. The koalas are all asleep. Curled up fluffily at the tops of trees or in the Y's of branches. Absurdly cute. Huge moorhens stalk about, pecking at the grass. Mewling little ducks with fluffy mohawks running down their necks. The Chocolate Drops café is doing a passable job of looking like an English tearoom and I buy some coffee from there and drink it on the veranda.

I would situate the moment at which I lost my fear of water here, in Yanchep, but the waiter tells me that the pool's gone, now. Its lining had eroded and the water was leaking into the basement of the nearby building so it was drained and filled in. Likewise the aviary; it was taken down to let the birds fly free. Which is pleasing news. The only animals in captivity here are the koalas, and they're happy in their trees, smashed out of their minds on eucalyptus. It comes back to me, suddenly, that Georgie the cockatoo was eventually given to this park. Is he still about? How long do cockatoos live for? Is that him there, up in that tree, screeching his beak off?

The tall trees roundabout, I remember them as saplings. They might be remembering the same thing about me. Yet another place that rings and echoes with the boy I was. Sometimes, here, it seems as if the older me on the other side of the world, in Wales and in Liverpool, needs revisiting; as if I've properly regressed, and the me that I am in Wales is becoming more and more distant. This isn't just touring Australia, this is touring a large and formative part of my life. I'm a tourist through my own childhood. Strange jaunt, this; I become more alien to myself with each passing day.

THEN

And people:

The Penns, with whom the boy's family has a feud, after his sister, Linsey, has a fight with their daughter. The Penn father tries to run the boy's father down when the boy's father is holding his tiny baby.

The Macleods – Nick, Tim, and Darren. The older one, Tim, our boy doesn't much like, but, despite the odd falling out, he remains friends with the other two. One day at a beach, Nick paddles far out to sea on a surfboard, so far that his screams can barely be heard. He thrashes back to shore, his skin even paler than its usual bone-white hue, his ginger hair standing, literally, on end. He babbles hysterically about a giant fish which swam up towards him with its mouth open and nudged the surfboard. His fear is infectious and our boy doesn't go in the sea that day.

The Rickards, who live opposite on Elizabeth Road, and who are a big family; not in numbers, but in size. The children especially. Big kids. Hefty. The boy is friends with Glen, who shows him, one day, how to fire a gidgee, which is a small trident attached to a rubber strap, used for spearfishing. Glen shoots the boy in the ear. Blood flows. Mr Rickard is a very funny man, and our boy likes him. One day the children paint sheets of wood for a treehouse or a den or something and Mr Rickard admires it. *Hell of a job* he says, stroking one particular piece. *Did you paint this one? No*, says the boy, *Glen did*, and Mr Rickard says: *Oh well he's made a shithouse job of it.* The boy finds this very funny. Glen will often walk along Elizabeth Road singing 'Hello Hawaii' over and over again.

The Johnsons, of the half-albino mother. Frank Giovanni, who, during school swimming lessons in the sea, panics and tries to use Tony as a flotation device. The instructor has to rescue Tony, someone else has to swim out and rescue Frank. Tony's first girlfriend, Mandy Knight, a West Ham fan. The boy and his brother and Gary Johnson would fish, with rods, for goldfish in the fountains outside the council offices. There's a boy called Duncan, extremely dependent on his mother; 'mummymummymummy!' is all he seems to say. An Italian family move in next door, and invite the boy to tea. He eats spaghetti for the first time, parmesan cheese, etc. He loves it. A whole new exciting world of gustatory discovery and pleasure is opened up to him. He watches a western where a horseman rescues a damsel by snatching her up with one arm onto his horse; he tries to do this with the youngest Italian girl, on his bike, and blacks her eye and bloodies her nose. There's a family from Huyton, in Liverpool – Lily and Jerry. Jerry works with the boy's father. He falls asleep in the sun one day and gets third-degree burns on his legs. Their boy leans on a table made from a log in our boy's front room and the table breaks in half. Jerry's son is upset and runs away home.

And our boy, one day, loses his fear of water. Up to now, he'd approached the stuff only when bedecked in armbands and rubber rings, but then one day, and quite without warning, it feels to him in some way like he is going home. It happens in Yanchep, in the pool, where he's gone with the school. He's snuck off to see Georgie the cockatoo in the aviary and then joined his class in the pool and without thinking he slips into the deep end, bobs for bit close to the wall, gets out and walks to the shallow end and slips in again. Their teacher is standing in water up to her chin with her legs wide and the children are plunging under, swimming through the arch of her legs and resurfacing; until now, the thought of such voluntary sub-mersion would've had the boy terrified but now he's under and through and up in a blink and rejoining the line of splashing kids to do it again. He'll forget, instantly, his hydrophobia, and soon he'll be snorkelling over reefs and rocks, marvelling at fish and squid. Soon he'll be seeking water out. Soon he'll wonder why he was afraid of it in the first place.

And places: The boy goes on a Boys Club trip to Guilderton, a campsite between the coast, north from Perth, and the Yeal Nature Reserve. The boys stay in log cabins surrounded by trees, the ideal setting in which to stay up late telling ghost stories, which they do, and in the early hours before dawn the boy and some of his friends creep over to the girl's cabin and make spooky noises outside the window and run away laughing when the girls start hollering. The boy discovers a large flattened area in the vegetation, as if some big animal had slept there, which gives rise to tales of beasts and bunyips in the woods.

He loves Guilderton, the boy. Loves the mist rising off the lake and the thick green woods. A steep hill runs down into the lake, down which has been built a small trackway; a kind of skateboard can be slotted into the trackway at the top and ridden down on. At the bottom it comes to an abrupt halt and catapults the rider into the lake. The boys ask the teacher if they can go on it. He says no, so they ask him until he says yes but the skateboard thing can't be found so the boys just leap shouting into the lake from the jetty instead.

The smell of the forest and the mysterious sounds behind the leaves. It's April 1978. Elvis Presley dies. The boy's mother, long a fan, is upset on the telephone. A dance is held in the campsite hall. Our boy gets invigorated on sugar and additives and watches a girl he knows, dressed as a squaw, doing the hokey-cokey. She's in his class at school and he's suddenly looking at her in an entirely new way. She spins around with her hands in an inverted steeple, cupping her chin, and the tassles on her skirt and the warpaint on her face draw and keep the boy's eye. He is eleven years old, not far off twelve, and is growing not smoothly but it seems in a series of jerks and jolts. When he walks across the dancefloor to the drinks table for another glass of orangeade of amphetamine-strength sugar content, he notices that he's walking in a new way, too – the rolling shoulders, the head back all haughty, the rippling hips. He's swaggering. Why is he walking in this way? He doesn't know. But he likes it. Thinks he might start walking like this more often.

NOW

Is this Guilderton? This is nothing like I remember it. Nothing
at all. Where's the lake and the trackway? Where are the
cabins? I go into the visitor's centre and explain what I'm
doing there and I'm given a number and told to ring it so I go
outside to a callbox and do and a lady answers and I explain,
again, what I'm doing in Guilderton and she tells me that the
log cabins have long gone and the place is given over now to
caravans and holiday cottages. I thank her and go for a walk
around. I'm by the sea, and I don't recall the place being
anywhere near the sea. I remember it inland, with thick green
trees and big foggy lakes. I don't recognise this at all. I'm
struck, here, by how erroneous our memories can be. How
events can mutate, with time, in the mind. And if that's true,
then how certain can you ever be about yourself, given that
you misremember drastically the events that made you the
person you are? This is a little bit alarming. So I don't think
about it. I remember Guilderton. The dancing girl and the new
way of walking.

We drive down to Quinn's Rocks. Rain and an angry sea.
Man-made rock outcrops on which I'd sit as a kid next to a
beach on which I'd walk with my dad. We don't stop long – the
weather's foul. But it sets us off singing 'The Mighty Quinn',
which becomes 'The Mighty Hig', made amusing by insulting
lyrics: 'He's got a penis / But it's not very big / You ain't seen
nothing like the Mighty Hig!'

–Get fucked, says Higgy.

We return to Wanneroo. Go into the Wanneroo Tavern,
where my dad and grandad once got drunk thirty years ago. We
play pool. Rain batters down outside. I think of my grandfather

here, still alive, and my dad, younger, younger even than I am now. As I'm outside smoking I receive a text. It's from my mum, 12,000 miles away, and reads: REMEMBER THE LAMP-SHADES FALLING OFF THE CAR ON THE NULLARBOR? I don't, no. Christ how peculiar this is; I'm here at forty in a pub where my dad and his dad got drunk and my dad was younger then than I am now and my grandad's been dead for twenty years and my mum's sending me a text message from the other side of the planet and time and space expands and shrinks quickly like a panting chest. How peculiar this is. This cannot be measured. I don't know what to do with this. I go back into the bar and drink a lot more.

THEN

The pains in the mother's legs get worse. They become crippling. The doctor can find nothing physically wrong with her.

Tony throws a pen up into the air one day and it lands nib-first in baby Nicola's fontanelle. She screams and holds her head and cries and shrieks uncontrollably and Tony collapses around his guilt. Nicola recovers, quickly.

Linsey has a friend, Nicola Crook, with whom she shoplifts from Cole's supermarket. Ten pairs of knickers and a jumper. They show their haul to Linsey's mother who is immediately suspicious. The boy watches.

–Where'd you get these from?

–At Cole's. They were throwing them away.

–Did you steal them?

Linsey thinks and frowns and then points at a pair of knickers. –We stole that.

Nicky Crook says –Tell the truth, Linsey, we stole them all.

The girls and their plunder are marched down to the supermarket. The booty's returned. The girls apologise to the displeased manager. Who remains displeased and mutters about the police although he doesn't actually contact them.

Children do this. They push and poke and prod at the world, at the limits of their location in it, they test the elasticity of their bonds to other people both known and unknown. This is healthy. This is what children should do. It is them stamping their personality on a world incomprehensibly vast and confusing. The boy understands this, even at that age, although it's not yet a thing he can articulate beyond the abilities of his body.

In May of that year, they go as a family to the television studios of Channel 7 to watch the gameshow *Family Fortunes* being filmed. Other families, friends, go with them. The boy finds it boring, but is excited when, during the interval, free Snickers bars are given out, but he's startled to find that a Snickers is exactly the same as a Marathon. What manner of adult trickery is this? What vile breed of antipodean chicanery? He's never thought that Marathons could be bought in Oz, and he's missed them, and now, after three bloody years... Plus 'Snickers' is a stupid name. He's gone without Marathons for three years now, and, as it turns out, needlessly so. Damn this bleeding country.

Back home, there's a bundle of rags on the outside porch. The father asks who left them there and gives them a kick and they shout. It's Terry Madigan, sleeping, another scouse feller come all the way from Brisbane to visit.

–You weren't in, he says, –and I was knackered.

–Yer daft sod.

Terry stays for a while.

And one day the boy is watching the news. The bemused newsreader is talking about a 'craze' in the UK called 'punk' and a band called the 'Sex... Pistols'. He fills the gap between the two words with a small smirk and a shake of his head and a bucket-load of contempt. A clip of the band is shown. The boy is enraptured in a second. They've made themselves look as ugly as possible but they're singing about how pretty they are and the lead singer appears to be some kind of hunchback, snarling and leering and grinning and spitting. The noise they make is ferocious and enraged, a calculated affront to the kind of people who would call the police on little boys gazing at their goldfish. An electric charge blasts and crackles through the boy. He feels like he's been woken up from a long sleep. Like a bucket of icy water has been thrown over him. He feels alive. The clip of the band is a short one and when the newsreader fills the screen again with his neat hair and trimmed muzzy and tie and tan and gob pursed and puckered like a dog's arse with lemon juice squeezed into it the boy wants the band back, wants to see more of them, hear and feel more of the marvellous noise that they produce. He knows now, suddenly and in an instant, what he wants to be, what he wants to do, when he grows up.

The mother's leg pains get worse.

NOW

It's June 28th. We get on the Rottnest Island ferry at Fremantle dock and immediately on the boat I hear 'The Mighty Quinn' on the cabin's radio. Haven't heard that song in years and *now* look. This is a sign. Of what? Rottnest is a holiday island, once a colonial barracks and prison; its main hotel was originally the summer residence of the Governor of WA. It has bars and restaurants and little cute animals called quokkas, rabbit-sized kangaroos, and I'm excited about going. It's that thing, again, about travelling over water. It exhilarates me and seems somehow to possess some mysterious depths of meaning and significance, even if the purpose of the trip is simply to get drunk and stroke small animals.

The ferry disgorges a load of students in sombreros and shorts and flip-flops, carrying boom-boxes and small barrels of Heineken. Loud and look-at-me-ish, like students the world over. I ponder on what might be a good collective noun for students; an arseache? A wick? A gobshite of students? Tony didn't come to Rottnest with me when I was a kid – I went with the school, I think – so I tell him about the quokkas, and how they gave the island its name (the early Dutch settlers thought they were rats, hence 'Rat Nest' = 'Rottnest'). Their defence against threat is to curl up into a ball; take that, and the employment of the island as a haven for pissed-up Aussies, and you get 'quokka soccer'. Nice.

It's a rough crossing. The ferry bucks and bounces on the sea like an angry stallion. Even this mad motion, I trust. Something about water, travelling over water. It feels right, to me. In the little harbour when we get off, a dolphin is throwing a big fish high into the air, catching it in its mouth, breaching out of the water, tossing the fish again, catching it again. Awesome and beautiful. This is nothing but play. The dolphin's behaviour is just a revelling. He's happy to be alive, that dolphin. A couple, older, are watching him with great glee and I get talking to them. They're Ten Pound Poms too, been in Oz for forty years, as long as I've been on the earth. He's from Leeds, she Somerset, with a mother from Tremadog. I like them. We watch, with a shared joy, the dolphin exult. I exult too.

The tourist office offers me and Tony accommodation at $30 a night. This is amazingly cheap. A full-sized bungalow – a balcony, several bedrooms, bathroom, kitchen, for thirty bucks a night. Even better, we're next door to a gaggle of gorgeous women, who are on their balcony drinking and dancing and laughing and not wearing very much. A century ago, this was a high-security prison for aboriginal miscreants. Now it's karaoke-capital. Some changes are to be applauded.

This is brilliant. I love this island. The quokkas are every-where, and so accustomed to human company that they'll approach you for a tickle. They swoop on the leftovers outside the cafés; I watch one pick up a chip in his wee paws and dip it into a bowl of ketchup before eating it. They hang around the bars, gazing longingly through the windows. They're entrancing to watch. We get on a bus to tour the island. The driver asks where we're from and we tell him that we live in Wales.

–Wales, ey? Play much rugby there or are ya still learning?

–Learnt quite a bit in four hundred years or so, mate.

–Didn't ya beat the Poms?

–Aye. During the Six Nations grand slam last year.

–In that case I'll only charge ya Aussie prices. Seven bucks.

I like this feller; I like his openness, I like the way he understands that Britain is not all Pommie-land. And he shows us great things; huge and hulking wrecks on the beaches, astounding rocks and cliffs. And then he points out an osprey's nest on a rock and asks us if we have ospreys in Wales and we tell him yes, there's a few breeding pairs recently returned, and he says:

–Yeh, but we look after our birds here. It's not like in the UK. Buggers don't steal their eggs here. Our birds are under protection.

–As they are in Wales, I say. –Twenty-four hour CCTV. Armed guards, in some places.

He doesn't seem impressed by this, or even convinced, and, even though I quite like this feller, I'm annoyed. Typical Oz attitude; everything we do is better. What, does he think that we have open season on our raptors in Britain? That we're allowed to shoot them, steal their eggs? Does he not think that we revere and respect our ospreys, just as they do on Rottnest Island? And this from the place that gave the world quokka soccer. Don't lecture me on how to look after our wildlife until you can look after your own. Jesus Christ.

And now I've had my fill of Australia. I'm sick of that general superciliousness, that smugness, and I'm sick, too, of the Brit ex-pats who have slavishly been taken in by it. I'm flying back to Brisbane tomorrow to catch a plane to Los Angeles and I'm looking forward to it. Want, now, to be out of Oz. I've had more than enough of the place. Glad I left when I did, at the age of twelve. Hate to think how I might've turned out, had I stayed. But I'm going to make the most of my night on Rottnest so I get drunk and tickle quokkas behind the ear until my index finger turns white.

THEN

The mother stays home with the baby and the father takes the three other children to a quiz night in the Wanneroo town hall. They come last, and win a cabbage. Tony's friend from school,

174

Warren Arbuckle, comes first. Ponce.

A travelling fair visits the district. It has a dunker stall; a man sits on a retractable plank over a tank of water and if you hit a bullseye with a ball the plank is whipped out from under him and he falls in the water. Tony hits the target. The feller's dunked. The watching crowd yell: *Give it to the Pommie with the dead-eye!*

Out in the bush one day the childen make a fire and cook damper; flour and water and raisins mixed and wrapped in foil and cooked in the embers. Linsey calls this 'spotted dick', and sets her tracksuit top on fire and runs away like a comet. She's unharmed, and the mother buys a patch in the shape of an 'L' and sews it over the burn-hole.

The father comes home from work one day with a mirror advertising Swan lager. A present, he says, because he's leaving the job. A few days later, on June 6th and after some frantic jettisoning of belongings, they drive out to the airport and board a plane for London.

NOW

–It was that sudden, was it?

–Don't you remember?, Tony says. –We were all shocked. No sooner had they told us we were going back and we were on the plane.

I have one last thing to do in Perth. I have to visit the Palm Court Reception Centre at the zoo on Labouchere Road, where we spent a Christmas day as kids. I don't recall anything about it, which might be just as well because it doesn't exist any more; it's now the Zoological Gardens Functions Room. Same building, though, and as I stand in front of it some recollections do trickle back; the plants, the huge and vivid flowers, the purplish colour of the building materials. I ate a Christmas dinner here, once. A long time ago.

We return to Fremantle. Get a room above a pub, a shit-hole of a room with half-drunk bottles of beer all over it and sheets that smell of someone else's sweat, opposite a brothel which stays open all night. I'm tired, so sleep through the pub hubbub, and we take the van back in the morning and get my deposit back and meet up with Higgy and get on the plane to Brisbane where Tony meets up with his pole-dancer who will, in a few weeks' time, reveal herself to be sadly approaching unhinged. I stay that night in a motel close to the airport and ask the owner where the nearest pub is and he answers 'about 9 km' and there is no taxi service in the area and even the external areas of the motel have signs saying 'NOBODY SMOKES HERE!', with a little smiley face, don't be maverick, be like us and we'll all get along just fine, do what we do and let's all be nice except I'm there and I *do* smoke and I can't believe there's not even a bar within walking distance and no fucking taxis to be had either so I just go to bed and in the early morning I fly to Los Angeles and that's it. I'm out of Oz. Sick to the gizzard of Oz.

COMING BACK

THEN

The plane leaves Australian airspace and the pains leave the mother's legs. As if they're umbilically linked to Australia; they stretch as the plane moves away from the country and eventually snap and are twanged back to Oz earth like severed hamstrings.

An age later they land in London and get on a train to Liverpool. The parents give each other a look as the train starts to slow at Edge Hill along trash-strewn railway tracks beneath a sky the colour of drain-water. On the platform at Lime Street, the mother's mother is there to greet them, wearing a headscarf and mac and holding a plastic bag. The father's face falls further.

And they grow and age and change. It is discovered that Nicola has a serious heart defect – due, maybe, to the travel-sickness pills which the mother took on the trek across the

Nullarbor – which needs to be treated with a big and invasive operation. She is in hospital for a long time, and the boy weeps when he sees her; tiny, octopus'd by tubes. But the operation is successful. The father discovers an off-licence on Myrtle Parade, close to the hospital, that sells his favourite Swan lager. The boy, in later years, will use this off-licence when staying with his girlfriend on Bedford Street South and when all goods in the shop are protected by smash-proof perspex and it is run by the most hilariously rude man the boy, or the young man he will then be, has ever met.

Jump to 2000. Nicola, a woman now, is working in Liverpool Museum. She is approached by a couple who ask her if she remembers them. They are Lily and Jerry. They last saw Nickie when she was an infant, and it is truly incredible that they recognise her now.

Five years or so later, there's an unexpected knock at the mother's and father's door. The dad opens it. There's Peter Higgins on the doorstep, Higgy, soon to become the Mighty Hig.

Soon after that, Nickie and her husband return to Australia, and New Zealand, for a long holiday. Shortly after that, Tony does the same thing with his second wife, soon to become his second ex. And shortly after that, I too go back. And, of course, return.

They grow, and age, and change.

NOW

The plane takes off at 11 a.m. I'm in the air for twelve hours and I land in Los Angeles at 7 a.m. the same morning. Hate long-hauls. I don't understand them. Some hours to kill in LA so I get a cabbie to drive me around and show me some sights and I'm unimpressed and then I board the plane to Vancouver and I'm utterly exhausted and the world swims and spins and Vancouver customs take over two hours to clear, the interrogation at the desk taking half an hour itself, and another cabbie drives me into a city of sparkling towers surrounded by huge and snow-veiled mountains and at a traffic light the driver of the next car has a tattoo on his arm which reads 'FILIPINO THRU N FUCKIN THRU' and I check into my hotel, the Quality Hotel at 1335 Howe Street, and sleep for a few hours then I go exploring and drinking and in the morning my pockets are filled with beermats and cigarette papers with various names and numbers scrawled on them by the lovely citizens of this lovely city which Dylan Thomas called 'a handsome hellhole' and which I grow to think of, affectionately you understand, as 'a stunning shitpit'. I'm in it for five days. I drink a lot and walk a lot in a kind of relaxed rush and slowly feel a very heavy weight lift off my shoulders and I gradually realise how glad I am to be out of Australia. It was getting to me, that country, and I don't realise how much so until I wake up on my second day in Vancouver and breathe a deep sigh of relief. I spend a lot of time gazing at the mountains and the inland sea. I explore Gastown and, again, narrowly miss a mugging on Hastings and Main. Glittering bigness of the city. Even the beggars are sweet: 'Good morning sir, and excuse me, but can I be a pain in the ass and trouble you for fifty cents?' I've been in Canada before, in Ottawa, and was a tad underwhelmed then, but Vancouver I love. I could stay here longer. It's not Australia.

I have a bulkhead seat back to London next to a sweet German girl, only eighteen, who'd just had a holiday in

Vancouver on her own, and we land ten hours later and I'm exhausted and the plane to Manchester is delayed three hours and then when I'm on it it sits on the tarmac for a further two and the flight itself takes twenty mere minutes and I think of asking the steward to ask the pilot if he can empty the shit-tanks over Old Trafford but don't and we land and I can hardly walk I'm so tired but there's my girlfriend who I haven't seen for seven weeks and we have a rib-cracking hug and my luggage has been lost but I'm past caring. We drive back to my parents' house and I go in and the first thing I say to them is: 'Thank *Christ* you brought us back from Oz'. And that's it.

But the weight of a long history is a good one to carry. I dwell on this as we drive back, the next day, to Wales. The castles, the hill-forts, the old houses, the standing stones and cairns on the mountain tops and in the green fields. A depth of human life is open and available here, at your shoulder, ready to hand, and there's a heft to it but it's a good weight to carry, like muscle or a favourite coat. Makes you feel part of a grand and epic story. And the seasons turn around you, here, come and come again, alternately turning your skin pink then brown, pink then brown. Measure your life in the appearance and disappearance of swallows.

At home, there's a parcel waiting for me; a copy of *Diary of a Welsh Swagman*. I'd tracked it down on-line in an internet caff in Vancouver. Thirty quid. I'd forgotten I'd ordered it. My eyelids are closing as if made of iron and it's all I can do to stay upright and my words are slurred and I don't feel good so I'll start reading it tomorrow, when I feel better.

ACKNOWLEDGEMENTS

I'm sure it's obvious from the text who I wish to thank by name, but further thanks must go to Tony, Higgy, Uncle Roy, my mum and dad, and Ian Peddie. Also to the many Aussies I know and love in that country and this, not least among them Pete Salmon and Kerry Watson of The Hurst.